AAT UNIT 4

Supplying Information for Management Control

STUDY TEXT AND WORKBOOK

Foundation (NVQ/SVQ Level 2)

ISBN 1 84390 327 X

British Library Cataloguing-in-Publication data

A catalogue record for this book is available from the British Library.

We are grateful to the Association of Accounting Technicians for permission to reproduce past assessment material. The solutions have been prepared by FTC Foulks Lynch.

Published by

FTC Foulks Lynch
Swift House
Market Place
Wokingham
RG40 1AP

Printed and bound in Great Britain

Contents

Preface

This is a study text and workbook for Unit 4 (Supplying Information for Management Control) of the AAT Foundation NVQ/SVQ Level 2 in Accounting.

Study Text

The study text is written in a practical and interactive style:

- ♦ key terms and concepts are clearly defined

- ♦ all topics are illustrated with practical examples with clearly worked solutions

- ♦ frequent practice activities throughout the chapters ensure that what you have learnt is regularly reinforced

- ♦ 'pitfalls' and 'examination tips' help you avoid commonly made mistakes and help you focus on what is required to perform well in your simulation.

Icons

Throughout the text we use symbols to highlight the elements referred to above.

   Key facts

   Examination tips and techniques

   Pitfalls

   Practice activities

Workbook

The workbook comprises three main elements

(a)   A question bank of key techniques to give additional practice and reinforce the work covered in each chapter. The questions are divided into their relevant chapters and students may either attempt these questions as they work through the study text, or leave some or all of these until they have completed the study text as a sort of final revision of what they have studied.

(b)   A practice simulation.

(c)   Two mock simulations which closely reflect the type of simulation students may expect.

Standards of Competence

Unit 4   Supplying Information for Management Control

Unit Commentary

This unit is about recognising and providing basic management information. This involves information relating to both costs and income and includes the comparison of actual costs and income against the previous period's data, the corresponding period's data and forecast data.

The first element involves recognising cost centres. It should be noted that in some organisations profit centres or investment centres will be used in place of cost centres, and these will differ depending on the organisation. The element also involves recognising elements of costs, coding income and expenditure and identifying and reporting obvious errors, such as the wrong code or excessive volumes. You are required to extract information relating to the three elements of costs: materials, labour and expenses. The element, however, does not specifically relate to manufacturing as materials will include items such as consumables in service industries and the majority of costs will probably be labour costs in those circumstances.

The second element is concerned with extracting information from a particular source, for example the previous period's data, and comparing that information with actual costs and income, in line with the organisational requirements. You are required to report discrepancies between the two in the appropriate format, ensuring confidentiality requirements are adhered to.

Elements contained within this unit are:

Element 4.1	Code and extract information
Element 4.2	Provide comparisons on costs and income

		Chapter
Knowledge and Understanding		
To perform this unit effectively you will need to know and understand		
The Business Environment		
1	Types of cost centres, including profit centres and investment centres *(Element 4.1)*	1
2	Costs, including wages, salaries, services and consumables *(Element 4.1)*	Throughout
Accounting Methods		
3	Identifying cost centres *(Element 4.1)*	1
4	The purpose of management information: decision making; planning and control *(Element 4.1)*	1, 8
5	The make up of gross pay *(Element 4.1)*	3
6	The relationship between financial and management accounting *(Element 4.1)*	1
7	Methods of analysing information in spreadsheets *(Element 4.2)*	10
8	Methods of presenting information, including word processed documents *(Element 4.2)*	6, 7, 9
9	Handling confidential information *(Element 4.2)*	6, 9
10	The role of management information in the organisation *(Element 4.2)*	1, 8
11	Awareness of the relationship between financial and management accounting *(Element 4.2)*	1
The Organisation		
12	Relevant understanding of the organisation's accounting systems and administrative systems and procedures *(Elements 4.1 & 4.2)*	9
13	The nature of the organisation's business transactions *(Elements 4.1 & 4.2)*	Throughout
14	The goods and services produced, bought and delivered by the organisation *(Element 4.1)*	Throughout
15	The cost centres within the organisation *(Element 4.1)*	Throughout
16	Organisational coding structures *(Element 4.2)*	1 - 5
17	The organisation's confidentiality requirements *(Element 4.2)*	9
18	House style for presentation of different types of documents, including word processed documents *(Element 4.2)*	6, 7

Unit 4　　Supplying Information for Management Control

Element 4.1　　Code and extract information

Range Statement

Performance in this element relates to the following contexts

Elements of cost

♦　Materials

♦　Labour

♦　Expenses

Sources

♦　Purchase orders

♦　Purchase invoices

♦　Sales orders

♦　Sales invoices

♦　Policy manual

♦　Payroll

Information

♦　Cost

♦　Income

♦　Expenditure

Errors

♦　Wrong codes

♦　Excessive volumes

Unit 4   Supplying Information for Management Control

Element 4.2   *Provide comparisons on costs and income*

Chapter

Performance Criteria

In order to perform this element successfully you need to

A	Clarify **information** requirements with the appropriate person	6, 9
B	Compare **information** extracted from a particular **source** with actual results	6 - 9
C	Identify discrepancies	8, 9
D	Provide comparisons to the appropriate person in the required **format**	6 – 10
E	Follow organisational **requirements for confidentiality** strictly	6, 9

Range Statement

Performance in this element relates to the following contexts

Information

◆　Costs

◆　Income

Sources

◆　Previous period's data

◆　Corresponding period's data

◆　Forecast data

◆　Ledgers

Format

◆　Letter

◆　Memo

◆　E-mail

◆　Note

◆　Word processed report

Confidentiality requirements

◆　Sharing of information

◆　Storage of documents

STUDY TEXT

CHAPTER 1

Principles of cost accounting

FOCUS

This chapter covers the following Knowledge and Understanding and Performance Criteria of the AAT Standards of Competence:

Types of cost centres, including profit centres and investment centres *(Knowledge and Understanding element 4.1)*

Identifying cost centres *(Knowledge and Understanding element 4.1)*

The purpose of management information: decision making; planning and control *(Knowledge and Understanding element 4.1)*

The relationship between financial and management accounting *(Knowledge and Understanding element 4.1)*

The role of management information in the organisation *(Knowledge and Understanding element 4.2)*

Awareness of the relationship between financial and management accounting *(Knowledge and Understanding element 4.2)*

Recognise appropriate cost centres and elements of costs *(Performance Criteria element 4.1)*

In order to cover these the following topics are covered:

♦ The accounts department

♦ Cost accounting

♦ Cost units and cost centres

♦ Profit centres and investment centres

♦ Cost classification

♦ Cost behaviour

Key terms	
Financial accounting	The production of an historic record of transactions presented in a standard format for use by parties external to the business.
Management accounting	The generation, presentation and interpretation of historic, budgeted and forecast information for use by management for the purposes of planning, control and decision making.
Cost accounting	The analysis of costs and revenues to provide useful information to assist the management accounting function.
Cost unit	An individual unit of product or service for which costs can be separately ascertained.
Cost centre	A location, function, activity or item of equipment in respect of which costs are accumulated.
Profit centre	An area of business for which both costs and revenues can be separately ascertained.
Investment centre	An area of business for which costs, revenues and net assets can be separately ascertained.
Direct costs	Costs that can be related directly to a cost unit or centre.
Variable costs	Costs that vary in direct proportion to the level of activity.
Fixed costs	Costs that vary with time, not activity level.

1 The accounts department

1.1 Introduction

Most business entities, whether large or small, generate large numbers of **different types of transaction**. To make sense of those transactions, they need to be **recorded, summarised and analysed**. In all businesses, it is the **accounts department** that performs these tasks.

1.2 Provision of information

From the raw data of the business's transactions, accountants provide **information for a wide range of interested parties**. Each party requires, however, slightly different information, dependent upon their interest in the business.

1.3 Financial accounting information

Accountants provide information to **external groups**, such as the owners of the business, the Inland Revenue and HM Customs & Excise. This information tends to be presented as financial accounts. Financial accounts are a historic record of transactions which tend to be presented in a standard format laid down in law. Such accounts are normally only produced once or twice a year.

Financial accounting could be described in simple terms as **keeping score**. Financial accounting is not, however, the only type of accounting. The other main type is management accounting, of which cost accounting is a major part.

 Financial accounts show a historic picture of what has happened to the business during the past accounting period. Financial accounts are largely for external users.

1.4   Management accounting information

The management accounting function of a business normally provides accounting information for **internal users**, such as the managers of the business. Management accounting compares actual results with predicted results and tries to use information to make further predictions about the future. It also provides information which managers can use to make decisions.

Management accounts can be produced in any format that is useful to the business and tend to be produced frequently, for instance every month.

1.5   The aim of management accounting

The aim of management accounting is to assist management in the following areas.

♦   **Decision making**

 Managers need information to assist in making decisions. These decisions will typically be about prices to charge for products, quantities to produce, the amount and type of material or labour to use etc.

♦   **Planning**

 Primarily through the preparation of annual budgets (short-term planning), but also through long-range strategic planning.

♦   **Organising**

 Planning enables all departments to be organised and to work together for the benefit of the entity. This avoids *lack of goal congruence*, ie individual managers who want good results for their department at the expense of the organisation as a whole.

♦   **Controlling**

 Comparing actual results with the budget helps to identify where operations are not running according to plan. Investigating the causes and acting on the results of that investigation helps to control the activities of the business.

♦   **Communicating**

 Preparing budgets that are distributed to department managers helps to communicate the aims of the entity to those managers.

♦   **Motivating**

 A tight but attainable budget communicated effectively should motivate managers (and staff) and improve their performance. If the target is too difficult, however, it is likely to demotivate and it is unlikely to be achieved.

 The main purpose of management accounting information is to provide the information management need for planning, controlling and decision making.

1.6   What is useful management information?

For **management information** to be of use to a particular group of managers, it must have the following attributes:

♦   **Relevant to their responsibilities**. For example, a production manager will be primarily concerned with information about stocks, production levels, production performance and machine loads within his particular department. He is not concerned with the problems of other departments unless they specifically affect his department.

♦ **Relevant to any particular decision**. Management must have the relevant information to be able to identify areas where decisions must be made and to make those decisions.

♦ **Produced on time**. Information has to be up-to-date to be of any value.

♦ **Valuable**. There is no benefit in producing information if it is not of value to the enterprise. If information is produced which has no effect on the decisions made by management, then it has no value to the business and should not be produced.

2 Cost accounting

2.1 Introduction

Cost accounting is usually a large part of management accounting. As its name suggests, it is concerned with **establishing costs**. It developed within manufacturing businesses where costs are most difficult to isolate and analyse.

Financial accounts give totals of costs and revenues. They do not show, for example:

(a)   the amount of costs and profit on each unit of product or each service provided

(b)   the amount of cost and/or revenue attributable to each manager

2.2 Cost accounting system

A **cost accounting system** must provide sufficiently detailed information concerning both historic and projected costs and revenues to enable analyses such as these to be carried out.

 Thus cost accounting is primarily directed at providing the **required information for management**, whether on a routine basis, or on an *ad hoc* basis to enable management to perform the functions of planning, control and decision making. To that end, cost accounting is concerned with:

(a)   determining costs and profits during a control period;

(b)   valuing stocks of raw materials, work in progress and finished goods, and controlling stock levels;

(c)   preparing budgets, forecasts and other control data for a forthcoming control period;

(d)   creating a reporting system which enables managers to take corrective action where necessary to control costs;

(e)   providing information for decision-making.

Items (a) and (b) are traditional **cost accounting roles**; (c) to (e) extend into **management accounting**.

2.3 Service industries

Cost accounting is not confined to the environment of manufacturing, although it is in this area that it is most fully developed. **Service industries, central and local government, and even accountancy and legal practices** make profitable use of cost accounting information. Furthermore, it is not restricted purely to manufacturing and operating costs, but also to administration, selling and distribution and research and development.

 Cost accounting is concerned with analysing costs and revenues in such a way that they are useful to management for the purposes of planning, controlling and decision making.

3   Cost units and cost centres

3.1   Introduction

An important part of the cost accounting function is the **identification of costs with individual areas of the business and with individual units of output,** whether a product or a service.

This **cost ascertainment** exercise allows greater control over costs than if they were kept in total terms (ie for the business as a whole) and gives valuable information for performance appraisal and decision-making.

Thus a business will need to define appropriate **cost centres** and **cost units** for which costs will be separately ascertained.

3.2   Cost unit

 A **cost unit** is an individual unit of product or service, for which costs can be separately ascertained.

The particular cost unit selected will depend upon the **type of business or activity** involved and the amount of information available.

Note that cost units can be defined for **productive** operations (eg a manufacturing business) where the unit will normally be defined in terms of physical output and for **service** operations (eg a professional firm or a service department within an organisation) where the unit will be defined in terms of the activity involved.

3.3   Examples of cost units

Some examples for different types of operation are given below:

Business	Cost unit
Car factory	1 car (of each model produced)
Brick-making	1,000 bricks
Brewing	Barrel
Electricity	Kilowatt-hour
Solicitors	Chargeable hour
Education	Enrolled student
Hotel	Bed-night
Transport company	Passenger-mile
Hospital	Patient-day

Service activity	Cost unit
Credit control	Account maintained
Personnel	Employee
Selling	Orders taken

Notes

(1)   The cost units given for each business/activity are only suggestions. There are often equally useful alternatives. For example, the cost unit for education could be a successful student, or a week's tuition course, whilst selling costs could be ascertained in respect of £ of turnover or calls made.

(2)   The last three examples in the business section are known as *composite cost units.* These are often used in relation to service businesses or activities, where cost is considered to depend upon more than one principal factor.

For the purposes of Unit 4 you will not be dealing with cost units, only cost centres.

3.4 Cost centre

A **cost centre** is a location, function, activity or item(s) of equipment in respect of which costs are accumulated.

A cost centre is therefore used as an **initial collection point for costs**. It is the collection of costs into appropriate cost centres which is the aim of Unit 4.

The **location, function or item of equipment** referred to in the definition can be related to production, organisation or to a service department or a service organisation.

3.5 Examples of cost centres

Examples of cost centres would include the following:

Nature of activity	Cost centres
Production organisation	Assembly line
	Packing machine
Service dept	Stores
	Canteen
	Quality control
Service organisation	Tax department (accountants)
	Ward (hospital)
	Faculty (college)

3.6 Responsibility for cost centres

Each will have a **cost centre manager** who will be held responsible for the control of costs within that centre. The performance of the manager will be partly assessed on their ability to meet predetermined budgets for costs (taking account of the level of activity achieved, as measured by the cost unit for that centre).

4 Profit centres and investment centres

4.1 Introduction

In the previous section cost centres were explained and illustrated. In some organisations there are not only cost centres identified but also profit centres and investment centres.

4.2 Profit centres

A profit centre is an area of the business for which both costs and revenues can be ascertained.

If the revenue of a part of the business can be determined as well as the costs of this part of the business then these two can be compared in order to determine the profit of that part of the business.

In some organisations areas such as the stores department or the selling function might be treated as profit centres rather than just cost centres.

4.3 Investment centres

An investment centre is an area of the business where costs, revenues and net assets can be ascertained.

Therefore an investment centre is not only an area of the business for which a profit can be ascertained by comparing revenues to costs but also the specific assets and liabilities of that part of the business can be identified. The profit can be compared to the net assets of the business in order to calculate a return on the net assets; this is the profit divided by the net assets expressed as a percentage.

In some organisations various divisions or physically separate departments may be treated as investment centres.

Profit centres are areas of the business for which both costs and revenues can be identified. Investment centres are areas of the business for which costs, revenues and net assets can be identified.

Activity 1 *(The answer is in the final chapter of this book)*

(AAT J94)

Suggest ONE suitable cost unit and TWO cost centres for a college of further education.

5   Cost classification

Costs can be **classified** (collected into logical groups) in many ways.   The particular classification selected will depend upon the purpose for which the resulting analysed data will be used, for example:

Purpose	Classification
Cost control	By type – materials, labour, expenses
Cost accounts	By relationship to cost units or cost centres.
Budgeting, decision making	By behaviour – fixed/variable costs

The first type of classification is self-explanatory and will also be dealt with in more detail in later chapters. The second two types are now considered in more detail.

6   Cost behaviour

6.1   *Variable costs*

Variable costs are those that vary (usually assumed in direct proportion) with changes in the level of activity of the cost centre to which they relate (eg output volume).

6.2   *Variable costs – example*

Material X is used in a product. If 1,000 units of the product are made then £5,000 of material X is used; if 2,000 units of the product are made then £10,000 of material X is used.

The variable cost per unit **may not remain constant over a wide range**. It may be possible in the above example to obtain discounts for large purchases of material, reducing the cost per unit.

6.3   *Fixed costs*

Fixed costs accrue with the passage of time and are not affected by changes in activity level. They are also known as **period costs**.

6.4   Fixed costs – example

Activity level	Hotel rent
1,000 guest-nights	£10,000
2,000 guest-nights	£10,000

6.5   Illustration of cost behaviour

The two different types of cost behaviour are illustrated below:

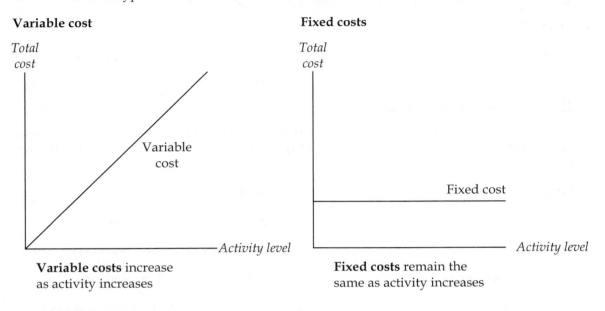

Variable cost

Fixed costs

Variable costs increase as activity increases

Fixed costs remain the same as activity increases

Activity 2 *(The answer is in the final chapter of this book)*

Which of the following best describes a 'pure' fixed cost?

A cost which:

A   represents a fixed proportion of total costs

B   remains at the same level up to a particular level of output

C   has a direct relationship with output

D   remains at the same level when output increases

---

7   Summary

In this introductory chapter a number of important issues have been raised. Firstly the relationship between financial accounting and management accounting was explained. Both accounting systems use the same information, the cost of materials purchased, cost of labour employed etc but each accounting system classifies and analyses the information in different ways to suit the purposes of each system. For the purposes of management information it is important that the information is in such a form that it can be used for decision-making, planning and control.

For the purposes of Unit 4 you are required to extract information from the relevant cost centres. Therefore it is important that you understand the meaning of cost centres, profit centres and investment centres.

8 Quick Quiz

1   Give three brief differences between management and financial accounting.

2   For a chain of department stores, give one possible example for each of a cost centre, profit centre and investment centre.

3   In general, would you expect the following costs to behave as variable or fixed?

   (a)   Management salaries

   (b)   Packaging

CHAPTER 2

Coding of costs and income

FOCUS

This chapter covers the following Knowledge and Understanding and Performance Criteria of the AAT Standards of Competence:

> Organisational coding structures (*Knowledge and Understanding*)

> Code invoice and expenditure correctly (*Performance Criteria element 4.1*)

In order to cover these the following topics are covered:

♦   Coding of accounting information

♦   Sales codes

♦   Example of sales codes

♦   Cost codes

Key terms	
Coding	A system of letters and numbers which uniquely identifies departments or cost centres or ledger accounts and which helps entry to the records, collation and analysis.
Sales codes	A coding system which uniquely identifies types of sales.
Cost codes	A coding system which uniquely identifies types of costs.

1   Coding of accounting information

1.1   Introduction

Cost accounting involves the **detailed analysis of costs** – between cost centres and cost units and between the various types of direct and indirect costs (labour, materials, production overheads, selling, administration, etc.).

To facilitate this analysis, a system of **coding** is likely to be devised by the organisation. As costs and revenues arise and are recorded within the cost accounts, they will be allocated a code according to the system set out in the costing system manual. For example, the purchases clerk enters the appropriate code on an invoice received for materials before passing it to the data processing department for input. Similarly, timesheets and other documentation used for the initial recording of labour time will generally have a space for coding.

Thus the costs are **analysed accurately and unambiguously at source**, allowing easy production of cost centre and product cost information.

1.2 Hierarchical systems

The most common coding structure is **hierarchical** with the detail of the classification built up from left to right by the individual digits within the code.

For example, the code for the cost of a manager's time spent on a particular client's work in a firm of solicitors may be recorded under a code built up as follows:

4	=	Conveyancing department
42	=	Direct cost (within the conveyancing department, etc.)
421	=	Chargeable employee time
4212	=	Managerial time
42123	=	Correspondence with client

This will allow **analysis of costs** to any level of detail required – by cost centre (using the first digit), by chargeable/non-chargeable time (using the third digit).

Codes will normally be entirely numerical, as these are processed more efficiently on a computer.

2 Sales codes

2.1 Introduction

Coding sales follows the hierarchical system described above, but generally each element of the code will have two or three digits allocated to it rather than the one in the previous example. This allows for expansion of the system. Thus, if the conveyancing department is just code number 4, and the business expands such that you need to distinguish between the 'conveyancing planning department' and the 'conveyancing operational department', the single digit code will not allow for this. But if conveyancing was set up as 40 or 400, then expansion is possible by allocating:

'Conveyancing planning department'	-	40 (or 400)
'Conveyancing operational department'	-	41 (or 401)

2.2 Typical sales codes – example

Let us consider a business which uses sales codes comprising three main categories of information:

Sales centres		Types of customers	
UK sales	100	Business	400
European sales	200	Individuals	500
Rest of World sales	300		

Types of product	
Garden machinery	600
Garden furniture	700
Plants	800

Produce the sales codes for the following transactions.

	Sales centre	Customer type	Type of product
(a)	UK	Business	Garden machinery
(b)	Europe	Individual	Garden furniture
(c)	UK	Individual	Plants
(d)	Rest of World	Business	Garden machinery

2.3   Solution

(a)   100   400   600

(b)   200   500   700

(c)   100   500   800

(d)   300   400   600

2.4   Commentary on solution

(a)   You may only have to deal with two categories rather than the three above. This is easier but follows exactly the same principles.

(b)   The coding information will usually be contained in the business's 'Policy Manual'.

2.5   More detailed codes

Often a main code category (eg 'Garden machinery – 600') will be sub-analysed into the different types of garden machinery. For example:

Garden machinery	600
Lawn mowers	610
Hedge cutters	620
Chain saw	630 etc

This gives additional flexibility. The business can either produce a total for all garden machinery by combining all codes starting with the number 6, or can produce totals for each individual type of garden machinery.

2.6   How the codes are used

The revenue codes will typically form the basis of the coding of the ledger accounts in the books of the business. Computer systems clearly make this process much easier. The various categories of codes enable the business to report the revenue in different ways.

In the example in 2.2, the business may decide to have nine different accounts for sales:

Account code		Brief description	
100	600	UK	Machinery
100	700	UK	Furniture
100	800	UK	Plants
200	600	Europe	Machinery
200	700	Europe	Furniture
200	800	Europe	Plants
300	600	Rest of World	Machinery
300	700	Rest of World	Furniture
300	800	Rest of World	Plants

Note the business has decided not to have separate accounts for business and individuals.

How might the business use its coding?

(a)   **The financial accounts**

The business may decide to only show the geographical sales in the financial accounts. This reduces the information in the financial accounts and makes them more manageable.

(b)   **Management accounts**

The company may use all nine accounts for its management accounts. These would form the basis of discussion with the various managers regarding the performance of their divisions.

For example, UK machinery sales revenue (100 600) could be considered alongside the costs of making those sales and the profit reviewed.

(c)   **Business/individual sales**

A separate report could be run to produce the value of business and individual sales. This would be helpful for the sales department when considering how to focus their sales efforts.

The fact that there is a coding category does not mean that there has to be an account in the ledgers for every code.

3   *Example of sales codes*

3.1   *Example*

Manton Manufacturing produces and sells crockery in the UK. It has divided the UK into four regions (England, Northern Ireland, Scotland and Wales) and sells three product types of crockery (Breakfast, Tea and Dinner settings).

The coding system is as follows:

Sales centres	Code
England	100
Northern Ireland	200
Scotland	300
Wales	400

Product type	
Breakfast	700
Tea	800
Dinner	900

What do the following codes describe?

(a)   100   700

(b)   300   900

(c)   200   800

(d)   400   700

3.2   *Solution*

(a)   Sales of Breakfast sets in England.

(b)   Sales of Dinner sets in Scotland.

(c)   Sales of Tea sets in Northern Ireland.

(d)   Sales of Breakfast sets in Wales.

4   Cost codes

4.1   Introduction

Cost codes follow the same general principles of coding as revenue codes. A business will select the categories of costs it wishes to report and allocate codes accordingly.

The 'main' code will be the cost centre identified as most appropriate to the business's requirements. These might typically be:

Cost centre	Code
Machine shop	100
Assembly	200
Finishing	300

Other codes could then be used to specify further cost categories that the business identified. For example:

Cost category	Code
Materials	600
Labour	700
Expenses	800

Thus, materials used in the machine shop would be coded:

    100   600

or, labour used in the assembly department would be:

    200   700

4.2   Example

Owen Ltd manufacture motorbike helmets.

Factories:

Slough	110
Leeds	111

Cost centres:

Machining	120
Finishing	121
Packing	122
Stores	123
Canteen	124
Maintenance	125
Administration	126

Type of expense:

Labour	200
Material	201
Expenses	202

The following is a list of costs related to the business activity. Code these using the structure above:

(a)   Slough factory, cleaning materials used in the canteen.

(b)   Slough factory, wages for stores personnel.

(c)   Leeds factory, metered power (electricity) for machining department.

(d)   Leeds factory, telephone account for administration.

(e)   Slough factory, labour for maintenance department.

4.3   Solution

(a)   110/124/201

(b)   110/123/200

(c)   111/120/202

(d)   111/126/202

(e)   110/125/200

Activity 1 *(The answer is in the final chapter of this book)*

The expenses of an international organisation are coded with a seven digit code system as follows:

First and second digits	-	location
Third and fourth digits	-	function
Final three digits	-	type of expense

Extracts from within the costing system are as follows:

Location	Code
London	10
Dublin	11
Lagos	12
Nairobi	13
Kuala Lumpur	17
Hong Kong	18

Function	Code
Production	20
Marketing	21
Accounts	23
Administration	24

Type of expense	Code
Factory rent	201
Plant depreciation	202
Stationery	203
Telephone	204
Travel	207
Entertainment	209

Examples of the codes are as follows:

Factory rent in Nairobi:	1320201
Stationery purchased in London office:	1024203

Task 1

State the codes for the following items:

(a)   Depreciation of plant in the Dublin factory.

(b)   Administration telephone costs incurred in Lagos.

(c)   Salesman in Hong Kong entertaining an overseas visitor.

Task 2

State two advantages of using a coding system for the classification of costs and revenues.

5   Summary

Coding is a very important part of any accounting system. It enables sales revenue and costs to be identified and analysed in a very flexible and accurate way.

6   Quick quiz

1   Define the term 'cost code'.

2   List three purposes of cost codes.

CHAPTER 3

Materials costs

FOCUS

This chapter covers the following Performance Criteria of the AAT Standards of Competence:

Extract income and expenditure details from the relevant sources *(Performance Criteria element 4.1)*

Code income and expenditure correctly *(Performance Criteria element 4.1)*

Refer any problems in obtaining the necessary information to the appropriate person *(Performance Criteria element 4.1)*

Identify and report errors to the appropriate person *(Performance Criteria element 4.1)*

In order to cover these the following topics are covered:

♦   The stores department

♦   The materials control cycle

♦   The stores record card

♦   Coding of documents

Key terms	
Purchase order	A written order for goods or services, sent by the customer to the supplier, detailing quantities, prices, expected delivery dates and contract terms.
Purchase invoice	A request for payment for goods or services delivered, sent by the supplier to the customer, detailing quantities, prices, delivery date and contract terms.
Stores record card	A record kept for each stock line, detailing receipts, issues and balance on hand, in terms of both physical quantities and monetary value.

1   The stores department

1.1   Function of the stores department

The stores or stock department is responsible for the receipt, storage, issue and recording of the raw materials used in the production process.

1.2   Receipt of goods

When raw materials are received from suppliers they will normally be delivered to the stores department. The stores personnel much check that the goods delivered are the ones that have been ordered, in the correct quantity, of the correct quality and in good condition.

1.3 Storage of materials

Once the materials have been received they must be stored until required by the production departments.

Storage of materials must be appropriate to their type. For example, foodstuffs must be stored at the correct temperature and wood must be stored in dry conditions. Storage should also be planned in such a manner that the correct materials can be accessed easily either manually or by machinery.

1.4 Issue of materials

When the production departments require raw materials for production, it is essential that the stores department can provide the correct quantity and quality of materials at the time they are required. This will require careful attention to stock control policies to ensure that the most efficient levels of stocks of raw materials are kept.

1.5 Recording of receipts and issues

In many organisations the stores department is also responsible for the recording of the quantities of raw materials that are received from suppliers and issued to the production departments. This normally takes place on the **bin cards**.

2 The materials control cycle

2.1 Introduction

Materials can often form the largest single item of cost for a business so it is essential that the material purchased is the most suitable for the intended purpose.

2.2 Control of purchasing

When goods are purchased they must be ordered, received by the stores department, recorded, issued to the manufacturing department that requires them and eventually paid for. This process needs a great deal of paperwork and strict internal controls.

Internal control consists of full documentation and appropriate authorisation of all transactions in, movements of materials and of all requisitions, orders, receipts and payments.

If control is to be maintained over purchasing, it is necessary to ensure that:

♦ only necessary items are purchased.

♦ orders are placed with the most appropriate supplier after considering price and delivery details.

♦ the goods that are actually received are the goods that were ordered and in the correct quantity.

♦ the price paid for the goods is correct (ie what was agreed when the order was placed).

To ensure that all of this takes place requires a reliable system of checking and control.

2.3 *Overview of procedures*

It is useful to have an overview of the purchasing process.

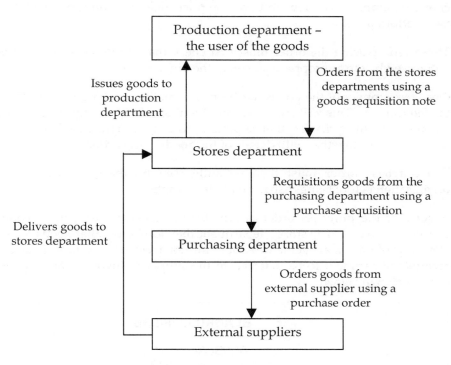

There are many variations of the above system in practice, but it is a fairly typical system and does provide good control over the purchasing and issuing process.

Activity 1 *(There is no answer to this activity in the final chapter of this book)*

Your organisation may have a slightly different process to this. See if you can draw a similar diagram illustrating the way your organisation's (or a familiar organisation's) purchasing process works.

(a)   **Goods requisition note**

The user department (eg a production department) will notify the stores department that it requires certain goods using a 'goods requisition note'. This note will be authorised by the production manager.

(b)   **Purchase requisition**

It is important that an organisation controls the goods that are ordered from suppliers. Only goods that are genuinely necessary should be ordered. Therefore, before any order for goods is placed, a purchase requisition must be completed.

Each purchase requisition must be authorised by the appropriate person. This will usually be the storekeeper or store manager.

When the purchase requisition has been completed it is sent to the purchasing department so that the purchase order is prepared.

(c)   **Purchase order**

Purchase orders will be placed with suppliers by the purchasing department.   The choice of supplier will depend upon the price, delivery promise, quality of goods and past performance.

The person placing the order must first check that the purchase requisition has been authorised by the appropriate person in the organisation.

Once the supplier of the goods has been chosen, the purchase price of the goods must be determined. This will either be from the price list of the supplier or from a special quotation of the price by that supplier.   The price agreed will be entered on the purchase order together with details of the goods being ordered.

The purchase order must then be authorised by the appropriate person in the organisation before being dispatched to the supplier.

A copy of the purchase order is sent to the stores department as confirmation of expected delivery. The stores department therefore know that goods are due and can alert appropriate management if they are not received.   A copy is also sent to the accounts department to be matched to the supplier's invoice.   An example purchase order is shown below.

BLACKHILL FILES

742 St Anne's Way
York   YO5 4NP

Telephone: 01904 27635
Registered in England, no 1457893

PURCHASE ORDER

Printing Unlimited   Order No: 35762
80 New High Street
Exeter   Ref: T Holmes
EX4 2LP

Date: 22 June 20X4

> Please print 25,000 labels at £10.50 from copy supplied per 1,000
>
> Needed by 20 July 20X4
>
> Payment within 30 days of delivery. 2% early settlement discount

Delivery to: As above

(d)   **Delivery note**

A delivery note is sent by the supplier to the stores with the goods being delivered.   This must include full details of the goods being delivered. The delivery note is signed by the person receiving the goods as evidence that the goods arrived.

(e)   **Goods received note**

When goods are received by the organisation they will usually be taken to the stores department rather than being delivered directly to the part of the organisation that will use the goods. This enables the receipt of goods to be controlled.

The stores department have copies of all purchase orders. It is important that the goods that arrive actually agree in **all** detail to those ordered before they are accepted.

When the goods are received, the stores department will firstly check what the goods are. They will be identified and counted and the supplier and purchase order to which they relate will be identified.

The details of the delivery note are checked to the actual goods and to the purchase order. It is important that the stores department checks that these goods were actually ordered by the organisation before accepting them.

Finally, when the stores department are satisfied with all of the details of the delivery, the details are recorded on a goods received note (GRN).

Any concerns about the goods being delivered (for example, too few, too many, the wrong colour, the wrong size) should be referred immediately to the appropriate manager before accepting the goods.

The GRN is evidence that the goods that were ordered have been received and therefore should be, and can be, paid for. The GRN will, therefore, be sent to the accounts department to be matched with the supplier's invoice.

As evidence of the actual receipt of the goods the GRN is also used for entering receipts of materials in the stores records.

VIBRANT LTD

GOODS RECEIVED NOTE   **No: GRN 272**

SUPPLIER: Slough Labels   DATE: 25/6/X3
                                 PURCHASE ORDER NO: TS 7921

DESCRIPTION	CODE	QTY	NO OF PACKAGES
AD Labels	TS 12	5,000	1

Received by: STORES – FINISHING AREA

Required by: FINISHING COST CENTRE 121

Accepted by: STORES SUPERVISOR

QUALITY ASSURANCE

Inspected by: SIG: ....

Qty passed: 5,000   **Qty rejected:**   Nil

(f) **Issues to the user department (production department)**

The circle is completed when the stores issues the goods to the production department. The goods must agree with the original goods requisition note.

(g) **Goods returned note - stores**

If goods are damaged or are not as ordered, they will be returned to the supplier. A goods returned note will be used, authorised by the stores manager.

Goods returned note – user department

When unused materials are returned from user departments to the stores, the transaction will be recorded on a document similar to the materials requisition but usually printed in a different colour. This will be a goods returned note. It will be completed by the user department that is returning the goods and signed by the storekeeper as evidence that the goods were returned to stores.

These returns must also be recorded in the bin card and stock ledger account.

When the goods are returned the details on the goods returned note must be checked to the actual goods themselves.

(h) **Purchase invoice**

The purchase invoice for goods details the amount that the receiver of the goods must pay for them and the date that payment is due. The purchase invoice might be included when the goods themselves are delivered, or might be sent after delivery.

The person responsible for payment must check that the details of the purchase invoice agree to the goods received note, the delivery note and the purchase order. This is to ensure that:

♦ what was ordered was received.

♦ what was received is what is being paid for.

♦ the price changed is that agreed.

Once it is certain that the purchase invoice agrees with the goods that were actually received then the invoice can be authorised for payment by the appropriate person in the organisation.

(i) **Credit notes**

If goods have been returned to the supplier, or there is some fault with the invoice (eg incorrect price or discount), a credit note will be requested from the supplier.

3 The stores record card

3.1 Introduction

When materials are received by the stores department, as we have seen, they will be immediately checked to ensure that the correct quantity and quality have been delivered. Once this has been done using the GRN then the details of the receipt must be entered into the stores accounting records.

3.2 Stores record card (bin card)

Every line of stock, eg component X and material Y, will have a record card showing precisely how much of this item is in stock. Therefore each time a receipt of a material arrives from a supplier then the stores record card must be updated.

A typical stores record card might look like this:

MATERIAL DESCRIPTION		Component X								
Code		X100								
Date	Receipts			Issues			Balance			
	Quantity	Unit price £	Total £	Quantity	Unit price £	Total £	Quantity	Unit price £	Total £

3.3 Quantity and price

In many management accounting systems only the quantity of the materials is entered by the stores department as that is the only information that they have. Therefore the copy of the stores record card that is held in the stores department will be for quantities only as this is the only information that is truly relevant to the stores department.

3.4 Accounts department

Once the stores record card reaches the accounts department then the correct price of the materials, taken from the purchase invoice, will be entered.

 The stores record card is an important document that helps to control the movement of materials and assess the stock levels of that material.

3.5 Stock ledger account

The accounting for material is dealt with through a **stores ledger account** (or a **stock ledger account**). This is maintained by the accounting unit. The physical stock shown on these accounts is reconciled with the bin card.

Definition A **stock ledger account** records the quantity and value of receipts and issues and the current balance of each item of stock.

3.6   **Example**

Vibrant Ltd has recently placed an order for 5,000 adhesive strips, showing the company logo, which are used on the company's range of products. It currently had 100 units in stock at a value of £25. The invoice from the supplier, Slough Labels Ltd shows:

Slough Labels Ltd
3 Station Unit
Slough SL1 3EJ

VAT No:	724371692
Tax point:	31 June 04

Tel: 01753 825431
Fax: 01753 825429
e-mail: Sloughlab@virgin.net

Invoice No: **72936**

INVOICE

To: Vibrant Ltd
       10 Royal Crescent
       Whitby YO21 3EA

Order No: 7921

Qty	Description	Unit price	Value £ p
5,000	Ad Label TS 12	£0.25 each	1,250.00
	VAT 17½		218.75
			£1,468.75

Terms: Net 30 days

Note:

This purchase invoice would be coded as:

110	/	121	/	201	£1,250.00
Slough Factory		Finishing cost centre		Direct material	

The Goods Received Note would be completed on receipt of the goods:

VIBRANT LTD			
GOODS RECEIVED NOTE			**No: GRN 272**
SUPPLIER: Slough Labels		DATE: PURCHASE ORDER NO:	25/6/X3 TS 7921
DESCRIPTION	**CODE**	**QTY**	**NO OF PACKAGES**
AD Labels	TS 12	5,000	1

Received by: STORES – FINISHING AREA

Required by: FINISHING COST CENTRE 121

Accepted by: STORES SUPERVISOR

QUALITY ASSURANCE

Inspected by: SIG: ....

Qty passed: 5,000   **Qty rejected:** Nil

The stock ledger card would be completed as follows:

STOCK LEDGER ACCOUNT

Material ....AD LABELS...   Maximum quantity ....

Code ....TS 12..   Minimum quantity ....

Receipts					Issues					Balance		
Date	GRN No	Qty	Price	Amount	Date	Material requisition	Qty	Price	Amount	Qty	Price	Value
										100	0.25	25.00
25/3	272	5,000	0.25	1,250.00						5,100	0.25	1,275.00

4   *Coding of documents*

4.1   *Introduction*

In order for all of the details considered earlier in this chapter to be entered correctly into the management accounting records it is vital that each document is correctly coded.

4.2   *Goods received notes*

The goods received note is used to write up the stores record card and therefore the actual stock item must be correctly coded. This is used for the entry for the amount of goods received.

4.3 Invoice

When the supplier's invoice arrives, this will detail the price of the goods received. Again this must be correctly coded so that not only the correct supplier's account is updated but the accounts department's stores record card can also have the unit price entered onto it.

4.4 Stores requisition

Where a user department requires stocks from the stores department then normally a goods requisition note will be filled out. This details the quantity of any stock item that is sent out to another cost centre. This must be correctly coded so that the correct stores record card is updated. This will be by quantity as well as by monetary value as determined by the organisation's policies.

 Once again the importance of correct coding of all materials movements cannot be stressed enough.

5 Summary

Materials costs can be a major cost of a manufacturing organisation. When materials are received they should be thoroughly checked to ensure that they have been ordered and that the correct quantity and quality have been delivered. Each receipt of goods must be entered into the stores record card in quantity initially and then with values added after the invoice has been received. When the goods are issued to the user departments or cost centres, the quantities will be recorded from the stores requisition.

6 Quick Quiz

1   What control procedure should prevent goods or services being paid for which have not been received?

2   What control procedure should prevent goods being requested from stores for an employee's own use?

3   How will a supplier's invoice need to be coded?

CHAPTER 4

Labour costs

FOCUS

This chapter covers the following Knowledge and Understanding and Performance Criteria of the AAT Standards of Competence:

> The make up of gross pay *(Knowledge and Understanding element 4.1)*
>
> Extract income and expenditure details from the relevant sources *(Performance Criteria element 4.1)*
>
> Refer any problems in obtaining the necessary information to the appropriate person *(Performance Criteria element 4.1)*
>
> Identify and report errors to the appropriate person *(Performance Criteria element 4.1)*

In order to cover these the following topics are covered:

♦ Paying employees

♦ Bonus schemes

♦ Sundry labour payments

♦ Timekeeping – recording and analysis

♦ Job analysis of gross pay

Key terms	
Piecework rates	Where a constant fixed amount is paid per unit of output.
Bonus scheme	A day rate combined with a bonus based on output achieved.
Timesheet	A record of how an employee has spent his/her time, split between jobs/clients and non-productive time.
Job cards	Records carried for each job/operation/client of time spent by employees on that job, materials used etc.
Wages analysis sheet	A record kept for each cost centre detailing the split of hours worked and payroll values between productive jobs and non-productive time for the purposes of charging labour costs to the appropriate accounts.

1 Paying employees

1.1 Introduction

Every employee of a business from the most senior management to the most junior member of the team will receive **remuneration**. How will this be paid? Common methods of payment include the following:

(a)   a **fixed salary** for a calendar period (week, month or year)

(b)   a **fixed amount per unit of attendance time** (eg. hour or day time rate)

(c)   a **fixed amount per unit of output achieved** (piecework rate)

(d)   a **combination** of a day rate and a bonus related to the output achieved (productivity bonus)

1.2 Piecework rates

Piecework rates occur where a fixed constant amount is paid per unit of output. The fixed rate will often be based upon the standard (expected) time per unit. This method is an example of 'payment by results'.

1.3 Example

Graeme MacHue works in the Scottish Highlands producing carved wooden animals for a small company supplying the tourist market. In week 26 his production was:

	Standard time allowed/unit
6 Stags	2.0 hours
5 Otters	1.5 hours
12 Owls	1.0 hour
6 Golden Eagles	2.0 hours

He is paid £5 per standard hour of production (irrespective of actual time worked).

What are his earnings for week 26?

1.4 Solution

		£
Stags	6 × 2 × £5	60.00
Otters	5 × 1.5 × £5	37.50
Owls	12 × 1 × £5	60.00
Golden eagles	6 × 2 × £5	60.00
		217.50

1.5 Advantages of the piecework system

♦   It produces a constant labour cost per unit.

♦   It **encourages efficient work** – an employee taking more than the standard time per unit will be paid for the standard time. In order for this to be motivational, the standard time must be accepted as fair by the employee.

1.6   Disadvantages of the piecework system

♦   Employees **lack security of income** which may become demotivating.

To help overcome this, a **differential piecework system** may be implemented, whereby the piece rate is increased for higher output levels.

♦   The employee can be **penalised** for low levels of production due to factors that are outside his/her control (eg machine break-down or faulty materials).

1.7   Guaranteed minimum payment

To overcome the disadvantages, the **straight piecework rate** may be accompanied by a **guaranteed minimum payment** (weekly or daily).

1.8   Example

Standard rate per hour = £4.50

Guaranteed minimum per week = 35 hours

Actual production: 10 units @ 3 hours per unit. Calculate the weekly pay.

1.9   Solution

Standard hours worked = 10 × 3 = 30 hours

Pay = 30 × £4.50 = £135

Subject to guaranteed minimum pay = 35 × £4.50 = £157.50

Therefore weekly pay = £157.50

Piecework is a method of remunerating employees where they actually produce specific items. In order to be motivational a differential piecework system may be used and to prevent employees suffering from factors that limit their production a guaranteed minimum may also be introduced.

Activity 1 *(The answer is in the final chapter of this book)*

A company operates a piecework system of remuneration. Employees must work for a minimum of 40 hours per week. Joe produces the following output for a particular week

Product	Quantity	Standard per item (hours)	Total actual time (hours)
Gaskets	50	0.2	9
Drive belts	200	0.06	14
Sprockets	100	0.1	12
Gears	10	0.7	6
			——
			41
			——

He is paid £4 per standard hour worked. What are his earnings for the week?

---

2 Bonus schemes

2.1 Introduction

Bonus schemes are a compromise between a day rate and a piecework system. Earnings will comprise:

(a) a **day rate amount**, based on **hours worked**; and

(b) a **bonus** based on **quantity produced** (usually above a certain standard) or on time saved in relation to standard time allowance for the output achieved.

2.2 Example

On a particular day, Fred worked for 8.5 hours, producing 15 units. The standard time allowance for each unit is 40 minutes. Fred's basic hourly rate is £4.50 and he is paid a bonus for time saved from standard at 60% of his basic hourly rate.

Calculate Fred's pay for the day.

2.3 Solution

		£
Day rate = 8.5 × £4.50		38.25
Bonus		
Standard time for 15 units 15 × 40/60	10 hours	
Actual time	8.5 hours	
Time saved	1.5 hours	
Bonus = 1.5 × £4.50 × 60%		4.05
Total		42.30

 The **benefit of time saved is shared between the employer and the employee**, in this case in the ratio 40/60. This method partially safeguards both the employee and the employer against badly set standards; it also safeguards cases where it is difficult to set accurate standards because of the nature of the work.

2.4 Group bonus scheme

In the case of, for example, an assembly line, where it is impossible for an individual worker on the line to increase productivity without the others also doing so, a **group bonus scheme** may be used. The bonus is calculated by reference to the output of the group and split between the members of the group (often equally).

3 Sundry labour payments

3.1 Introduction

As well as the normal payments of wages and salaries, there are various other labour costs that will need to be incorporated into the costing system. These would include **overtime, holiday pay, and training time**.

3.2 Overtime

Overtime can arise from working outside normal hours, including weekends and bank holidays.

Overtime is usually paid at **some rate over the normal** (time and a half or double time). The excess over the normal rate is **overtime premium**.

Whether the overtime premium is charged to a particular job or to production overheads depends upon the circumstances under which it arose. For example, if it was necessary to complete a job in a shorter time scale as requested by the customer, it will be chargeable to that job.

3.3 Holiday pay

Holiday pay is non-productive, but it is nevertheless charged to the cost of production by allocating the full year's holiday pay to overhead and charging it to production for the whole year.

Alternatively, wages may be allocated at **labour rates inflated to include holiday pay** and other non-productive time costs.

3.4 Training time and supervisors' wages

Wages paid during a period of **training** may be charged partly to the job and partly to production overhead. The fact that learners work more slowly than trained employees is offset by the learners' lower rate of pay. Apprentices' remuneration will be charged to a separate account.

Normally, **supervisors' wages** are treated as part of department overhead unless only a particular job is concerned. Where instruction is being given, the remuneration of instructors and supervisors may be included in training time.

The gross pay of an employee can be made up of a variety of elements. Firstly, the basic remuneration, be it piecework, hourly rates etc must be calculated. Then any additional elements, such as bonuses and overtime, must be included to reach the total gross pay. This gross pay is the cost to the organisation of this employee (usually increased in the UK by the requirement to pay employers' National Insurance).

4 Timekeeping – recording and analysis

4.1 Recording

In most businesses, **records** are needed of the time spent by each worker in the factory (attendance time) and time spent on the operations, processes or products in the factory (job time). Such timekeeping provides basic data for statutory records, payroll preparation, ascertainment and control of labour costs of an operation or product, and statistical analysis of labour records for determining productivity.

Attendance may be recorded by using a **register**, in which employees note their times of arrival and departure, or by means of a **time recording clock** which stamps the times on a card inserted by each employee. Alternatively, employees may be required to submit periodic **timesheets** showing the amounts of normal and overtime work; these may also include job times as described below.

4.2 Job time bookings

Job time bookings can either be done manually or by the use of a time-recording clock; the method adopted will depend on the size of the organisation and the nature of the work, a clock being more suitable when there are numerous jobs performed each day.

4.3 Daily timesheets

One of these sheets (see below) is filled in by each employee (to indicate the time spent by them on each job) and passed to the cost office each day. The total time on the timesheet should correspond to the time shown on the attendance record. Because times are recorded daily, there is less risk of times being forgotten or manipulated, but these timesheets create a considerable volume of paperwork.

Daily timesheet

Name:	Frank Spencer			Date:	11/6/X5	
Clock Number:	3			Week number: 31		
		Time				
Job order number	Description	Start	Finish	Hours worked	Rate	£
349	Servicing Mini Metro GRS510W	9.00	11.05	2.05		
372	Repair to Austin Maestro BCD548A	11.05	16.30	4.25		
Signed: *F Spencer*		Certified: *A Foreman*		Office ref:		

4.4 Weekly timesheets

These are similar to daily timesheets but they are passed to the cost office at the end of the week instead of every day (although entries should be made daily in order to avoid error). Weekly cards are particularly suitable where there are few job changes in the course of a week.

4.5 Job cards

Here a card is prepared for each job or operation on which is recorded the time spent on that job by the employee concerned. Job cards also carry instructions to the operator as to how the job is to be carried out; this information normally comes from the planning department. Job cards lend themselves to mechanical accounting systems and reduce the amount of writing to be done by the employee, thereby reducing the risk of possible error.

4.6 Route cards

These are similar to job cards, except that they follow the product through the works and include details of all operations to be performed. They thus carry the cost of all operations on a job, which is useful for control purposes.

 In order to record and calculate the labour cost of an employee detailed and accurate records of the work performed will often be required. The accurate recording of attendance is also important for ensuring that each employee is paid the correct amount.

 Activity 2 *(The answer is in the final chapter of this book)*

(AAT D93)

(a)   List two advantages of paying employees by the results achieved.

(b)   Give two reasons why the majority of employees are paid on the basis of time (eg hourly rates of pay).

---

5 Job analysis of gross pay

5.1 Introduction

Where it is required to identify wages or salaries with particular jobs, contracts or processes, then in addition to their attendance records the employees concerned will have to keep **job time records**, either a card or slip for each job on which they work or a daily or weekly timesheet listing the various jobs. Such records should be scrutinised and approved by a foreman or other manager. When a bonus system is in operation, the record will also show the time allowed for each job.

The accounts department will reconcile the job time bookings for a period with the recorded attendance times, any discrepancy being investigated and if appropriate being treated as **'idle time'**. The job time records may include bookings both to customer work and to 'non-productive' work – for example, supervision, waiting time and machine cleaning. Sometimes, a separate time booking form or card will be used to record non-productive time.

In this type of instance the cost centre would be regarded as an individual job.

5.2 Recording of labour costs

After reconciliation, the various job and non-productive hours will be summarised and valued at rates which will ensure the **clearance of the gross pay which has been debited to the payroll control account** – commonly at the average effective pay rate for each group of employees calculated from the relevant payroll.

The **accounting entries** will be:

Debit (1) accounts for the various jobs

(2) expense accounts for non-productive times (overheads)

Credit Payroll control account

5.3 Wages analysis sheet

A simple form of wages analysis sheet for the above purpose is shown below:

WAGES ANALYSIS SHEET

Department: Assembly   **Week ended:** 17.5.XX

Average hourly rate: £5.25

| Employee | Productive work | | | | | | | Non productive | | | Total |
| Clock No. | Job No. 10 | | Job No. 15 | | Job No. 17 | | Job No. 21 | | | | hours |
	Hrs	£	Hrs	£	Hrs	£	Hrs	£	Code	Hrs	£	
1214	12	63.00	8	42.00			16	84.00	107	4	21.00	40
1215			15	78.75	15	78.75	10	52.50				40
1216	30	157.50	10	52.50								40
1217	25	131.25			8	42.00			102	7	36.75	40
1218			12	63.00	20	105.00	4	21.00	107	4	21.00	40
Total hours	67		45		43		30			15		200
Total amount		351.75		236.25		225.75		157.50			78.75	1,050.00

If an organisation produces a number of large individual products eg, buildings, aeroplanes, etc, then each product or job will be a cost centre in itself.

Activity 3 *(The answer is in the final chapter of this book)*

(AAT J93)

(a)   What is the purpose of a timesheet in a job costing organisation?

(b)   Why would an organisation want to record its hourly paid employees' hours of attendance?

Activity 4 *(The answer is in the final chapter of this book)*

(AAT J94)

(a)   Calculate the gross wages earned for each of the following employees for week 32. The normal week is 38 hours and an individual production bonus of 10p per 100 sheets produced is paid.

		Singh	Smith
Basic rate per hour		£4.50	£4.00
Total hours worked		39½	41
Overtime hours paid:	at time plus a third	1½	1
	at time plus a half		2
Output (sheets)		10,500	10,900

(Calculations to two decimal places of a £.)

(b)   There has been some pressure from the employees for a piecework system to be introduced.

What would the piecework price per 100 sheets have to be, to at least equal the gross wages earned by Singh in (a) above, assuming the same output level of 10,500 sheets?

(Calculations to two decimal places of a £.)

6   Summary

The gross pay of employees is a major cost to most organisations. This gross pay can be determined on a variety of different bases:

♦   annual salary

♦   weekly wage

♦   timed rate - per hour worked

♦   piecework – per product produced

♦   overtime payments

♦   bonus schemes

7 Quick Quiz

1   What is the purpose of a guaranteed minimum payment?

2   If the standard time allowed for a unit is 12 minutes, the basic hourly rate is £6.40 and an employee is paid a bonus for time saved from standard at 50% of basic rate, how much bonus would be earned by an employee who produced 27 items in four hours?

3   If overtime is worked as a result of an electricity failure in a factory during normal working hours, how would the corresponding labour costs be accounted for?

4   What will be the source of labour cost entries to job cost ledger accounts and overhead accounts?

CHAPTER 5

Expenses

FOCUS

This chapter covers the following Performance Criteria of the AAT Standards of Competence:

Extract income and expenditure details from the relevant sources *(Performance Criteria element 4.1)*

Code income and expenditure correctly *(Performance Criteria element 4.1)*

Refer any problems in obtaining the necessary information to the appropriate person *(Performance Criteria element 4.1)*

Identify and report errors to the appropriate person *(Performance Criteria element 4.1)*

In order to cover these the following topics are covered:

♦   Categorisation of expenses

♦   Revenue and capital expenditure

♦   Depreciation

♦   Types of expenses

♦   Accounting for expenses

Key terms	
Capital expenditure	Expenditure on the purchase or improvement of fixed assets, appearing in the balance sheet.
Revenue expenditure	Expenditure on goods and services that will be charged to the profit and loss account.
Expenses	Items of expenditure that are not labour or materials related.
Depreciation	An annual internal charge to the profit and loss account that spreads the net cost of a fixed asset over the number of years of its useful life.

1 Categorisation of expenses

1.1 Introduction

The previous chapters concerned the detailed recording of materials and labour costs. All other costs that might be of concern to the cost accountant could loosely be described as **expenses**. These can be analysed in various ways, depending upon their nature or relationship to cost units.

1.2 Categories of expense

The main categories of expense with which you need to be familiar are as follows:

♦ **revenue** and **capital** expenditure

♦ **depreciation** charges arising from capital expenditure

2 Revenue and capital expenditure

2.1 The basic difference

Capital expenditure relates to the purchase of fixed assets, that will appear on the balance sheet; **revenue expenditure** relates to expenses that will be charged in the profit and loss account.

2.2 Capital expenditure

Capital expenditure is expenditure incurred in:

(a)   the acquisition of fixed assets acquired for use in the business and not for resale

(b)   the alteration or improvement of fixed assets for the purpose of increasing their revenue-earning capacity

2.3 Revenue expenditure

Revenue expenditure is expenditure incurred in:

(a)   the acquisition of assets acquired for conversion into cash (ie goods for resale)

(b)   the manufacturing, selling and distribution of goods and the day-to-day administration of the business

(c)   the maintenance of the revenue-earning capacity of the fixed assets (ie repairs, etc.)

In practice, there can be some **difficulty** in clearly distinguishing between alteration/ improvement of fixed assets (capital) and their maintenance (revenue). For example, is the installation of a modern heating system to replace an old inefficient system an improvement or maintenance? However, you should not need to make such decisions at this stage.

Capital expenditure is expenditure on fixed assets that will be recorded in the balance sheet. Revenue expenditure is all other expenditure of the organisation that will be recorded as an expense in the profit and loss account.

2.4   The accounting treatments

Capital expenditure is charged to profit and loss over a number of periods, via the depreciation charge (see later in the chapter).

Revenue expenditure is generally charged to the profit and loss account for the period in which the expenditure was incurred.

The exception to this is the carrying forward of expenditure on items that remain in **stock** at the end of the accounting period.

2.5   The relevance of the distinction to cost accounting

Cost accounting is mainly directed towards gathering and analysing cost information to assist management in planning, control and decision-making.   In particular management are interested in:

(a)   the determination of **actual and forecasted costs** and profits for a period and for individual cost centres

(b)   the valuation of **stocks** (raw materials, finished goods, etc.)

Thus **revenue expenditure** is of far greater relevance to the cost accountant than capital expenditure. The main impact of capital expenditure on the above will be the depreciation charges that arise and that may be charged as a direct cost (as in the depreciation of machinery or equipment used in production or provision of a service) or split between various cost centres (depreciation of buildings, motor vehicles, etc.). Depreciation is dealt with below.

3   Depreciation

3.1   Introduction

The principles and computations for **depreciation** are covered in detail at the Intermediate level. However, you are expected to be aware of the basics as part of the expenses element of Unit 4.

3.2   Purpose of depreciation

When a fixed asset is bought, it is usually expected to be **kept and used within the business for a number of years**. At the end of this period, it will be disposed of – either scrapped or sold at a price usually below the original price.

♦   The amount of the original purchase price that is not recovered on the disposal of the asset represents a **cost of the use of the asset** and should therefore be charged as an **expense** of the business.

♦   The asset will have been used to the business's benefit over several years and thus the cost of its use should be **spread over the same period**.

Thus the purpose of depreciation is to provide a **systematic method** of spreading the 'depreciable amount' (cost less disposal proceeds) over the 'useful life' of the asset (how long the business intends to use it for).

3.3   Methods of depreciation

There are two main methods for calculating the amount of depreciation to be charged in each year of the asset's useful life: **straight-line method** and **reducing balance method**.

3.4   Straight-line method

This method provides for an **equal amount to be charged each year**; the annual charge would be calculated as:

$$\frac{\text{Cost} - \text{Disposal proceeds}}{\text{Years of expected useful life}}$$

3.5   Reducing balance method

A **percentage** is applied each year to the asset's net book value or NBV to calculate that year's depreciation charge. **NBV** is the original cost of the asset less the cumulative total of depreciation charged over its life to date.

The depreciation rate is expressed as a percentage and the annual charge under this method is calculated as:

$$\text{Net book value at the start of the year} \times \text{Depreciation rate}$$

3.6   Example

A delivery van is purchased for £6,000 cash. It is expected to be used within the business for four years, at the end of which it will be sold in part-exchange for a new one, with an expected trade-in value of £800.

Calculate the annual depreciation charges over the next four years using (a) the straight-line method and (b) the reducing-balance method at a rate of 40%.

3.7   Solution

(a)   The annual charge under the *straight-line method* will be:

$$\frac{£6,000 - £800}{4} = £1,300$$

(b)   £

	£
Cost	6,000
Depreciation Year 1 @ 40%	(2,400)
NBV	3,600
Depreciation Year 2 @ 40%	(1,440)
NBV	2,160
Depreciation Year 3 @ 40%	(864)
NBV	1,296
Depreciation Year 4 @ 40%	(518)
Final NBV	778

 The **straight line method,** as its name suggests, leads to **equal depreciation charges** each year. The **reducing balance method** leads to **high charges in early years** (when NBV is high) and lower charges later on (when NBV is lower).

3.8   Choice of depreciation method

Management may choose whichever depreciation method they think **most appropriate** for each type of asset.

4   Types of expenses

4.1   Introduction

An organisation will incur many different types of expenses. There may be expenses associated with the manufacturing process or the factory, the selling process, general administration or day-to-day running of the business and the financing of the business.

4.2   Manufacturing expenses – examples

Examples of expenses incurred during the manufacturing process are:

- Sub-contractor's costs.
- The power for the machinery.
- The lighting and heating of the factory.
- Insurance of the machinery.
- Cleaning of the factory and machines.
- Depreciation of the machinery.

4.3   Selling expenses – examples

When selling goods to customers the expenses that might be incurred are:

- Advertising costs.
- Depreciation of packing machine.
- Costs of delivering the goods to the customer.
- Commission paid to salesmen.
- Costs of after sales care.
- Warehouse rental for storage of goods.

4.4   Administration expenses – examples

The everyday running of the organisation will involve many different expenses including the following:

- Rent of buildings.
- Business rates on buildings.
- Insurance of the buildings.
- Telephone bills.
- Postage and fax costs.
- Computer costs.
- Stationery.
- Costs of providing a canteen for the employees.
- Auditor's fees.

4.5 Finance expenses – examples

The costs of financing an organisation might include the following:

♦ Loan interest.

♦ Lease charges if any equipment or buildings are leased rather than purchased.

Activity 1 *(The answer is in the final chapter of this book)*

(AAT J94)

A PC costing £3,000 was expected to last for four years and to have a resale value then of £200. The company policy is to depreciate assets using the straight-line method of depreciation.

(a) What is the annual depreciation charge to the administration cost centre?

(b) The computer was replaced after three years with no resale value. Calculate the obsolescence charge and state where this charge should be shown in the cost accounts.

---

5 Accounting for expenses

5.1 Allocation to cost centres

For control purposes, all costs eventually need to be **allocated to cost centres**. For materials and labour costs, this may be achieved by use of coded materials requisitions or analysed timesheets. The same principle will apply to expenses, although the allocation of joint (indirect) expenses may be done in stages.

The general approach to expense recording and allocation will be as follows.

5.2 Documentation

Most expenses will be documented by way of a **supplier's invoice or bill**. The authorisation for payment, codings for posting to the appropriate ledger accounts/cost centres and other internally added information may be attached by way of:

(a) a standard **ink stamp** with appropriate boxes for manual completion, or

(b) a **posting slip** stapled to the invoice.

Expenses that are internally generated (eg depreciation charges) may be recorded via a **journal entry** raised by the cost accountant, which will be coded appropriately.

 Again, in order for expenses to be charged to the correct cost centre, it is important that all expenses are correctly coded.

6 Summary

In this chapter the third category of costs was considered, expenses. In just the same way as with materials and labour costs the costs must be correctly coded so that they can be allocated to the correct cost centre.

One further topic that was introduced in this chapter was that of depreciation. This is a method of writing off the cost of a fixed asset over its useful life to the organisation. You do not need to know much detail of the accounting for depreciation, only to realise that it is a cost of the organisation and as such the journal entry that records the depreciation must be correctly coded to ensure that the appropriate cost centres are charged with their portion of the depreciation expense.

7 *Quick Quiz*

1 Is the purchase of stock capital or revenue expenditure?

2 If a computer cost £2,100, and is expected to be replaced after three years, when it can be sold for recycling for £400, what will be the second year's deprecation charge under the reducing-balance method at a rate of 42%?

CHAPTER 6

The sales function

FOCUS

This chapter covers the following Performance Criteria of the AAT Standards of Competence:

> Extract income and expenditure details from the relevant sources *(Performance Criteria element 4.1)*

> Code income and expenditure correctly *(Performance Criteria element 4.1)*

In order to cover these the following topics are covered:

♦ The sales department

♦ Sales income

♦ The sales department as a profit centre

Key terms	
Sales order	Internally raised documentation of an accepted order from a customer, detailing the goods/service ordered, agreed prices, terms of delivery and payment etc, sent to accounts, despatch and stores.
Sales invoice	Sent to the customer as a request for payment, with similar details to those of the order.

1 The sales department

1.1 Introduction

Most organisations will have some sort of sales department. This could be a retail outlet where goods are sold to the public or to trade customers. Alternatively the organisation may have an entire department which takes orders over the telephone, by post or by Internet from customers. Or a further alternative is that the organisation has a team of travelling sales representatives who take orders from customers and then transmit those orders back to the head office of the organisation.

1.2 Selling function costs

As with all other departments of the organisation the selling function will probably be distinguished as a cost centre. All of the costs associated with this function must therefore be coded and allocated to the cost centre as we have seen in earlier chapters.

1.3   Types of cost

One of the main costs of the selling function will tend to be labour costs, whether this is a team of administrators within head office dealing with sales, the sales staff in a shop or a team of travelling sales representatives. When determining the labour cost care should be taken with commissions. Many sales personnel will be paid a commission based either on the quantity or value of the sales that they make. These commissions must be correctly recorded as part of gross earnings of the employees and coded as a cost of the selling function.

If a force of travelling representatives is maintained then they are likely to incur travelling expenses such as petrol costs and the cost of overnight accommodation.

The sales department will also normally share a number of other expenses with other cost centres such as telephone, electricity, rent and rates etc.

One further specific cost of the sales function might be advertising costs which again must be correctly coded as a sales cost centre cost when the invoice is received.

 The sales function can be described as a cost centre in just the same way as the production cost centre or canteen cost centre. Therefore costs incurred by the sales cost centre must be correctly coded to ensure that they are correctly allocated and apportioned.

2   Sales income

2.1   Introduction

So far in this Textbook we have only considered the costs of the organisation. When sales are made then income is being earned.

2.2   The sales order

Apart from retail outlets, the sales process will start with the raising of a *sales order*. This will be prompted by the receipt of a purchase order from a customer, as discussed in a previous chapter. Stocks will be checked, as will credit limits for the customer. Provided the goods are available and the customer's credit level that will result is acceptable, the order will be accepted and a sales order raised (often on the computer), including product codes, description, prices etc. This will be conveyed to the stores/despatch department, where stock levels will be adjusted and goods packed for despatch.

For a service sales order (eg for the servicing of an appliance) the necessary time will be booked out to the customer.

2.3   The sales invoice

Once the goods have despatched or services rendered, a *sales invoice* will be raised which will be sent to the customer (representing their purchase invoice, as discussed previously). A copy will be used to record the sales income.

2.4   Different sales departments

In some organisations the sales department may be split into different areas, for example geographical or product group areas. If each area is a separate profit centre then it is important that the sales invoices are carefully coded to show which area or product group the sale relates to.

3 Sales department as a profit centre

3.1 Introduction

We have seen how the costs of the sales function must be allocated to it. However, in some organisations the selling function may be treated as a profit centre as it earns revenues as well as incurring costs. If this is the policy of the organisation then the sales invoices must be coded to ensure that this income is credited to the sales department and is then netted off against the costs of the department.

3.2 Cost of goods sold

The selling department is selling the goods that have been made by the organisation which in themselves have a large cost, the cost of actually manufacturing them.

In some organisations the sales function may be charged with this cost of the goods that they are actually selling in order to give a fairer picture of the profit of the sales profit centre. This will often be a standard (budgeted) cost figure, so that any efficiencies/inefficiencies of production do not affect the performance measure of the sales function.

3.3 Example

Information is given below about the selling function of an organisation for the month of June:

	£
Net value of sales (ie net of VAT)	277,600
Labour cost	86,400
Salesmens' commission	11,500
Salesmens' expenses	7,800
Other expenses	53,200
Manufacturing cost of goods sold	111,000

You are required to calculate the profit of the sales profit centre for the month.

3.4 Solution

		£
Sales		277,600
Less:	Manufacturing cost of goods sold	(111,000)
	Labour cost	(86,400)
	Commission	(11,500)
	Salesmens' expenses	(7,800)
	Other expenses	(53,200)
Profit for the month		7,700

 If the sales function is to be treated as a profit centre then it will be credited with the income from the sales made. It will also normally be charged not only with its own expenses but also with a standard cost figure for the goods actually sold.

Activity 1 *(The answer is in the final chapter of this book)*

Figures for the sales department of your organisation for the last month are given below:

	£
Salesmens' salaries (gross)	43,200
Salesmen's commissions	3,100
Salesmens' expenses	5,800
Head office sales team wages (gross)	21,600
Head office sales team expenses	6,700

During the month 110,000 units of the organisation's products were sold at a sales value (including VAT at 17.5%) of £550,000. The estimated manufacturing cost of the product is £3 per unit.

If the sales department is to be treated as a profit centre determine the profit that the department made for the month.

4   Summary

As well as considering costs you should be aware that information regarding sales income is also useful management information. This information can be obtained by treating the organisation's sales function as a profit centre.

5   Quick Quiz

1   Can you think of a type of commercial organisation that might not have a separate sales department?

2   Why do you think that a sales order is raised internally rather than simply using the customer's purchase order?

3   Why is it better for the sales department, if treated as a profit centre, to be charged with the budgeted cost of goods sold/services rendered rather than the actual cost?

CHAPTER 7

Methods of reporting information

FOCUS

This chapter covers the following Knowledge and Understanding and Performance Criteria of the AAT Standards of Competence:

Methods of presenting information, including word processed documents *(Knowledge and Understanding element 4.2)*

Handling confidential information *(Knowledge and Understanding element 4.2)*

House style for presentation of different types of documents, including word processed documents *(Knowledge and Understanding element 4.2)*

Clarify information requirements with the appropriate person *(Performance Criteria element 4.2)*

Provide comparisons to the appropriate person in the required format *(Performance Criteria element 4.2)*

Follow organisational requirements for confidentiality strictly *(Performance Criteria element 4.2)*

In order to cover these the following topics are covered:

◆ Form of reports

◆ Memo, letter or short report

◆ E-mail

Key terms	
Report	An orderly and objective communication of factual information eg by formal written document, letter, completed form, memo or spoken presentation
Memorandum report	Internal communication, often on standardised stationery, for routine reporting.
Fixed format report	Of a fixed length and style eg insurance claims, customer questionnaire.
Formal report	Findings of more complex investigations, generally including sections giving an introduction, approach to the investigation, detailed findings, conclusions and recommendations.
E-mail (electronic mail)	Messages, letters or reports sent electronically from the sender's computer to that of the recipient(s).

1 Form of reports

1.1 Introduction

Reports have five different **functions** as follows:

- informing

- analysing

- evaluating

- recommending

- describing.

1.2 Types of reporting

Reports can take **many forms** and can vary in length and status from:

(a)   **simple reports** in memo, letter or short report form; to

(b)   **fixed format reports**, such as accident reports; to

(c)   reports on **internal matters within a company** which may be formal or informal; to

(d)   **formal reports**, such as the findings of public enquiries.

2 Memo, letter or short report

2.1 Introduction

Many written reports in industry are **simple reports** concerning day-to-day problems and these tend to be short and informal. As such, they have a short life and are intended for only a few readers who are familiar with the problem and its background. The reader will generally be interested in the findings of the report and any action it will lead to.

Of the conventional short forms of informal report, three in particular deserve special attention: **the short report**, the **letter report** and the **memorandum report**. These will vary widely in form and arrangement, depending on the purpose for which they have been written.

2.2 The short informal report

This is generally only a **two or three section report**. The main areas are:

(a)   the name of the person requesting the report;

(b)   the title;

(c)   an introduction, which may also give the background;

(d)   the procedure, information, findings and 'overview' of the problem;

(e)   the conclusion;

(f)   the name and position within the company of the writer; and

(g)   the date.

The following example shows the basic structure but may be adapted to suit different requirements.

2.3   *Short informal report – example*

To: D Fagen

Date: 29 July 20X6

Subject: *Accounts Department reaction to proposed hot drinks vending machine installation*

Introduction

This report describes the reaction of staff in the Accounts Department of the Kenilworth branch office of Teck Bros to a proposal to replace existing tea and coffee-making arrangements with a hot drinks vending machine. The report was prepared on the instructions of D Fagen, Branch Manager and written by J Ely, Office Junior, Accounts Department. Instructions to prepare the report were received on 24 July 20X6 and it was submitted on 29 July 20X6.

Procedure

It was decided to interview personally all twelve members of staff in the Accounts Department. All staff were notified in advance. Questions were devised, three to establish staff reactions and a fourth inviting comments. All staff were then interviewed and the results noted. (A copy is appended to this report.)

Findings

(a)   In response to the question 'Would you be happy to see a vending machine installed?' EIGHT people said Yes, THREE said No and ONE was uncertain.

(b)   In response to the question 'Are you happy with the present arrangements?' THREE people said Yes, EIGHT people said No and ONE appeared unconcerned.

(c)   In response to the question 'Would you like to have a wider range of hot drinks available to you?' EIGHT people said Yes, THREE people said No and ONE was uncertain.

(d)   Amongst the comments made when staff were invited to comment on the proposal were 'Will fixed times for coffee and tea breaks disappear?' 'What about the tea ladies?' and 'I would prefer to obtain drinks at my own convenience'.

Conclusion

A clear majority of the staff (two-thirds) are in favour of this proposal.

J Ely
Office Junior
Accounts Department

2.4   *The letter report*

As the name implies this is a report written in **letter form**. It is used primarily to present information to or by someone outside the company. For example, an outside consultant may write his analysis and recommendations in the form of a letter, signing the letter as normal.

2.5   Memorandum reports

Memorandum reports are used primarily for routine reporting within an organisation, although some companies use them for external communicating. Because they are internal communications, they are often written on standardised inter-office memorandum stationery.

Following the company's identification or logo, if there is one, the words *To, From* and *Subject* appear at the top of the page. Sometimes the date is also part of the heading. Like letters, the memorandum may carry a signature or the writer may merely initial the heading.

2.6   Example

The business supplies buyer of Datewise Mr Hopkins has asked one of his clerks to investigate the costs and supply of 108mm × 219mm white envelopes, with a view to finding a cheaper source. In the role of the clerk, write a memo to Mr Hopkins explaining your findings.

2.7   Solution

Memorandum

To: Mr Hopkins

From: A Clerk   **Date:** 4 January 20X7

Subject: **Supply of envelopes**

As requested I have investigated the local suppliers of 108mm × 219mm white envelopes and compared the costs.

There are three main office suppliers to choose from: Paper Products, Office Treasures and Bestbuy.

Our current supplier, Bestbuy, has free delivery and offers us a 25 per cent discount on orders over £100.

Paper Products offer boxes of 1,000 envelopes £3 cheaper than Bestbuy on orders of six or more boxes. They offer the same discount and have a free delivery once a fortnight in this area. Special deliveries carry a charge of £20.

Office Treasures offer the same price as Paper Products but, as we would be new customers, they will not discuss discounts.

Paper Products would be most suitable for us as we always order more than six boxes and rarely need special delivery. I would recommend them for future supplies of these envelopes.

 As well as providing the information required, any form of report should usually include some form of conclusion from that information.

2.8   Reports on internal matters

The length and style (formal or informal) of reports produced and circulated internally will vary with the subject matter.

Some reports may be written to a strict brief but others may serve a **variety of functions**. In some situations, a whole string of reports may be produced as the result of one initiative.

For example someone may be asked to gather some **information** and to write it up in a report; they may then be asked to analyse that information and to write an **analytical report**; they may then be asked to make certain **recommendations** based upon the analysis and to write those up into a report.

2.9 Formal reports

Formal reports (such as the findings of public enquiries) may be internal or external to the organisation and are used for the more complex and important investigations commissioned by senior management.

In general, they will include the following:

(a) **introduction**, including terms of reference and background to the report;

(b) **approach to the investigation**;

(c) detailed **findings** (some of which may be presented as an Appendix);

(d) **conclusions** and **recommendations**, as appropriate.

You will need to be able to provide information that is required of you to the appropriate person in the organisation in the most appropriate format given the policies of your organisation.

3 E-mail

3.1 Introduction

Most large organisations are now fully computerised and employees can therefore communicate with each other via electronic mail or e-mail.

3.2 Methods of communication

An e-mail can be in the form of a letter, a memo, a short report or even a formal report. Whatever the procedures for the type of report these still apply to an e-mail.

However, great care must be taken to preserve confidentiality where necessary. It is far easier for e-mailed memos etc to be read by the wrong people, through being inappropriately copied/forwarded or being left on screen.

Activity 1 *(The answer is in the final chapter of this book)*

What would be the most appropriate method of reporting in each of the following situations?

(a) Reply to a query from a customer regarding the price of a product.

(b) Information for the finance manager on possible alternative suppliers of a material used in production.

(c) Analysis of salary costs of each different department of the organisation for the last five years required by the managing director.

(d) Reply to a colleague regarding petty cash policy.

---

4 Word processed documents

Some of the skills required for reporting information will require the use of word processed documents. These are dealt with at the end of Chapter 10.

5 Summary

For Unit 4 you will be required to report various elements of management information. Whenever asked to provide management information, you should always check precisely what is required and in what format.

6 Quick Quiz

1   What is the principal object of any report?

2   Give four sections that might appear in a formal report.

CHAPTER 8

Methods of presenting information

FOCUS

This chapter covers the following Knowledge and Understanding and Performance Criteria of the AAT Standards of Competence:

> Methods of presenting information, including word processed documents *(Knowledge and Understanding element 4.2)*

> House style for presentation of different types of documents, including word processed documents *(Knowledge and Understanding element 4.2)*

> Compare information extracted from a particular source with actual results *(Performance Criteria element 4.2)*

> Provide comparisons to the appropriate person in the required format *(Performance Criteria element 4.2)*

In order to cover these the following topics are covered:

◆ Tables

◆ Diagrams

◆ Bar charts

◆ Rules for drawing charts and diagrams

◆ Graphs

Key terms	
A one-way table	Summarises data by one characteristic (eg customers' ages, invoice values etc).
A two-way table	Summarises data by two characteristics (eg invoice by age and value).
A pictogram	A simple diagram which uses pictures to represent numbers.
A pie chart	A circle divided up into segments, each proportionately representing a category of data.
A simple bar chart	Represents each category of data by a bar, whose height or length is proportionate to the size of the category.
A component bar chart	A simple bar chart with each category bar being proportionately split horizontally into sub-categories or components.
A percentage component bar chart	Represents data presented in percentage form and has category bars of equal height, representing 100%, which are each proportionately split horizontally into sub-categories or components.

A compound (multiple) bar chart	Each category is represented by a set of sub-category bars whose height or length is proportionate to the size of the sub-category.
A graph	A diagram representing the relationship between two variables, x and y, represented on the horizontal and vertical axes respectively.
A time series	A series of figures measured at regular time intervals eg monthly sales, annual populations.

1 Tables

1.1 The purposes of tabulation

Most methods of data collection will result in **large amounts of data** being available. These large amounts of data will need to be examined to obtain relevant information. This means we must discard any irrelevant details, usually leaving us with a number of categories and sub-categories from which we wish to obtain some overall impression. The data remaining from the elimination of irrelevant details can be summarised using either **narrative** or **tables**.

1.2 Narrative v tabular

A **major drawback of the narrative approach** is that the information required is not clearly presented and only a limited amount of data can be presented. A properly constructed table, however, gives the required information immediately and clearly.

If information is to be useful to management then it must be presented in such a way that it is clear, unambiguous and understandable. Tables can help with this.

1.3 Example

A major bank is interested in the types of account held by its customers. The information below has recently been collected.

A sample of 5,000 accounts was taken, each account belonging to a different customer. 729 accounts were held by customers aged under 25 of whom 522 held current accounts, the remainder holding ordinary deposit accounts. 1,383 of the accounts were held by customers aged between 25 and 44, 1,020 being current accounts, 271 were ordinary deposit accounts and the remainder were high-interest deposit accounts. There were 1,621 accounts belonging to customers aged between 45 and 59, of these 61 per cent were current accounts, 29 per cent were ordinary deposit accounts and 10 per cent high interest deposit accounts. Of customers aged 60 and over, 628 held current accounts, 410 held ordinary deposit accounts and the remainder held high interest deposit accounts.

Here the data on the 5,000 accounts has already been examined and irrelevant details on, for example, sex of customer or length of time the account has been open have been eliminated. We are thus left with a reasonable amount of data and, by reading the narrative a few times, we are able to gain some useful information. The main drawbacks, however, in using this approach to present the data are:

(a)   What if the two eliminated variables, sex of customer and age of account, are considered relevant? This would make the narrative much longer and more cumbersome.

(b)   What if other categories were included (for example, an investment account)? This would have a similar effect to (a).

(c)   Perhaps we might like to make comparisons with another major bank or a similar sample of customers. We would then have two pieces of narrative to consider.

These points highlight the problems of using solely a narrative approach and hence point us to the **benefits of tabulation**.

1.4   *Solution*

Reconsidering the above example we will work through the **process of constructing a single table to summarise all the information contained in the narrative**.

(a)   **A simple one-way table**

A major point of interest in the given data is obviously the age breakdown of account holders. Working through the narrative, this could be presented as follows:

Age	*Number of customers*
under 25	729
25–44	1,383
45–59	1,621
60 and over	1,267

The figure for the 60 and over group is given by 5,000 – (729 + 1,383 + 1,621) since there are a total of 5,000 accounts each held by different customers.

(b)   **Title and headings**

The table in (a) gives us a clear breakdown of the ages of the customers but leaves the reader to guess what the columns mean. Clearly the left-hand column is age but it is better to label both columns clearly and to tell the reader what the subject of the table is. Also it is useful to show relevant totals, ie in this case the total number of accounts.

An improvement on the table given in (a) is thus as follows:

Ages of customers in a sample of 5,000 accounts

Age	*Number of customers*
under 25	729
25–44	1,383
45–59	1,621
60 and over	1,267
Total	5,000

(c)   **Another one-way table**

The data also informs us of the number of accounts held of each type. A table of this information is more difficult to extract from the narrative and some steps of working may be helpful.

(1)   There are three types of account: current accounts, ordinary deposit accounts and high interest deposit accounts.

(2)   Current accounts:

522 (age under 25);

1,020 (aged 25–44);

989 (aged 45–59; 61 per cent of 1,621 accounts = 0.61 × 1,621 = 988.81 or 989 accounts by rounding to nearest whole number of accounts);

628 (aged 60 and over).

(3)   Ordinary deposit accounts:

207 (aged under 25; ie 729 minus the number of current accounts = 729 – 522);

271 (aged 25–44);

470 (aged 45–59; 29 per cent of 1,621 accounts = 0.29 × 1,621 = 470);

410 (aged 60 and over).

(4)   High interest deposit accounts:

0 (aged under 25; we must assume this since no other detail is given);

92 (aged 25–44; 1,383 minus the number of current and ordinary deposit accounts = 1,383 – (1,020 + 271) = 1,383 – 1,291);

162 (aged 45 – 59; 10 per cent of 1,621 accounts = 0.10 × 1,621 = 162.1 or 162);

229 (aged 60 and over; total aged 60 and over minus number of current and ordinary deposit accounts = 1,267 (from (a)) – (628 + 410) = 229).

Summing the number of accounts in (2) to (4) gives the required table.

Number of different accounts held

Type of account	*Number of customers*
Current	3,159
Ordinary deposit	1,358
High interest deposit	483
Total	5,000

(d)   **A two-way table**

Our objective at the start of this paragraph was to construct a single table to summarise all the information contained in the narrative. Having carried out the simple calculations in (c) above, this is now easily done by employing a two-way table (sometimes called a cross-tabulation). In this example the two 'variables' are obviously age of customers and type of account held. These become the headings for the following required two-way table.

Ages and types of account held by sample of 5,000 customers

Type of account	*Age*				
	under 25	*25–44*	*45–59*	*60 and over*	*Total*
Current	522	1,020	989	628	3,159
Ordinary deposit	207	271	470	410	1,358
High interest deposit	0	92	162	229	483
Total	729	1,383	1,621	1,267	5,000

1.5   Guidelines for constructing tables

There are no set rules for constructing tables since tables often vary markedly in content and format. The following **guidelines** should however be adhered to:

♦   Always give the table a **title** and suitable **headings**.

♦ If the data contains a number of categories or sub-categories, use a **two-way table**.

♦ Give column and row **sub-totals** where appropriate.

♦ If the draft table contains too much detail, it will fail in its objective of summarising the data. **Further simplified tables** should then be constructed, each dealing with different aspects of the data.

♦ It is important to state the **source of the data**. This may be included in the title or given beneath the table.

♦ The **units in the table** should be 'manageable'. This can be accomplished by, for example, dividing particular column entries by 1,000 and including this fact in the column heading.

♦ It is sometimes useful to show **percentages** in the table in addition to the actual figures.

In analysing large amounts of data, tables similar to those already considered prove very useful. However, it is often the case that the data is in such a basic form (raw data) that using tables of this type is not easy.

Constructing a useful table is not as simple as you might initially imagine but the guidelines given above should help. Note that the use of computer spreadsheets can simplify the tabulation process, as illustrated in Chapter 10.

1.6   Example

Smith plc manufactures bed linen. In 20X2 its total sales were £126,000 and these sales increased by £28,000 in 20X3 and then again by £41,000 in 20X4. In comparison Brown plc, one of Smith's competitors, had total sales of £206,000 in 20X2 and their sales reduced by 10 per cent each year in 20X3 and 20X4. Present this information in tabular form.

1.7   Solution

(a)   It is useful in any problem where construction of a table is required to first write down the headings in the table. In this example this is easy:

Year	Sales of Smith plc	Sales of Brown plc

(b)   The next stage in problems of this kind is to work out the individual entries in the table:

Smith plc:	20X2	£126,000
	20X3	£126,000 + £28,000 = £154,000
	20X4	£154,000 + £41,000 = £195,000
Brown plc:	20X2	£206,000
	20X3	£206,000 – (0.1 × £206,000) = £206,000 – £20,600 = £185,400
	20X4	£185,400 – (0.1 × £185,400) = £185,400 – £18,540 = £166,860

(c)   The draft table is now easily formed:

Year	Sales of Smith plc £	Sales of Brown plc £
20X2	126,000	206,000
20X3	154,000	185,400
20X4	195,000	166,860

(d)   Since the units are all of the same order of magnitude, we can make the units more manageable by dividing by 1,000 and it might be acceptable to round Brown's figures to the nearest £'000. Also a title should be added to the table. The final table might thus have the form:

Sales of Smith plc and Brown plc for 20X2 – X4

Year	Sales of Smith plc £'000	Sales of Brown plc £'000
20X2	126	206
20X3	154	185
20X4	195	167

Activity 1 *(The answer is in the final chapter of this book)*

The total number of employees of Bunny and Hutch Ltd on 31 December 20X4 was 3,984, of which 2,124 were men. During 20X4, 221 men had been engaged and 185 resigned. The corresponding figures for women were 97 and 108 respectively. Because of the different types of work done, the average wage rate paid to male employees in 20X4 was £121.32 and to female employees £87.93. The company worked for 50 weeks in 20X4. Tabulate this data, including in your table an estimate of the total wage bill.

2 Diagrams

2.1 Basic charts

Charts and diagrams are frequently used to present data in a **clear and eye-catching way**. Large masses of complicated data can be presented in such a way as to be readily understood. There are many different charts and diagrams which can be used. The choice depends on:

(a)   the **type** of data;

(b)   the **amount** of data;

(c)   what factors should be **emphasised**, if any.

You should always ensure that the end result is a chart or diagram which is clear and intelligible. If drawing by hand, you should always use a ruler. Charts and diagrams can also be produced from computer spreadsheet software, as discussed in Chapter 10.

Remember that charts and diagrams give visual information for comparing relative size. As such, they are unsuitable for conveying precise numerical information. Where precision is required, tables of data should be used.

2.2 Pictograms

A pictogram is a simple diagram which uses pictures to represent numbers. Suppose we have the number of letters received by mail-order firms in the following table:

Firm	Annual number of letters
Great Galaxy	3,475,000
Commonwealth	8,122,000
Largeforests	5,108,000
Ells	4,427,000
Berties	6,381,000

We could use a picture of a letter to represent a number of actual letters. In this case if we use a picture of a letter to represent 1,000,000 letters received, we obtain the pictogram shown below.

Annual number of letters received by mail order firms

Key: Represents 1,000,000 letters

✔ Always remember to include the **key** on your diagram.

As can be seen, fractions in the pictogram are difficult to show accurately, but that is not the purpose of these diagrams. They are to give us a **quick, rough idea of relative size** and as such are fairly successful.

2.3   Example

Draw an appropriate pictogram for the following beer sales figures.

Brewery	Quarterly sales figure £
Soprano	542,000
Blackdough	397,000
Empties	56,000
Browns	315,000

2.4 Solution

(Probably the easiest picture to use is a glass of beer.)

Quarterly beer sales figures for four breweries

Soprano

Blackdough

Empties

Browns

= £100,000 sales per quarter

 Pictograms are very inexact but they do give an immediate impression of the data being portrayed.

2.5 Pie charts

A **pie chart** consists of a circle split into segments. The circle represents a total and the segments represent the parts which go to make up the total. The 360° of the circle is divided in proportion to the figures making up the total.

2.6 Example

Suppose a family's income in 20X5 is £1,000 per month, and their expenditure splits down as follows.

	Amount £	Proportion %	Angle (degree)	
Mortgage and insurance	300	30	108	(30% × 360)
Electricity and gas	50	5	18	(5% × 360)
Food and drink	200	20	72	etc
Clothes	40	4	14	
Car and petrol	150	15	54	
Telephone	10	1	4	
Savings	70	7	25	
Fares	60	6	22	
Miscellaneous	120	12	43	
	1,000	100	360	

Draw a pie chart to illustrate this.

2.7   Solution

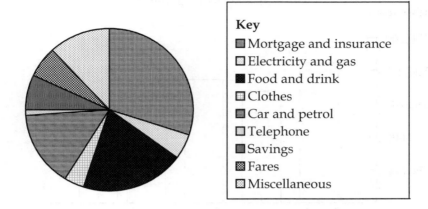

Key
- ▦ Mortgage and insurance
- ☐ Electricity and gas
- ■ Food and drink
- ▦ Clothes
- ▦ Car and petrol
- ☐ Telephone
- ▦ Savings
- ▩ Fares
- ▦ Miscellaneous

You can either use the names in the segments or represent each category by a different colour or shading, provided a key is given. Again, we do not obtain a precise idea of expenditure on certain items or services, just an idea of their **relative proportions**.

 A pie chart is quite complicated to produce because of the angles but it does give a good visual impression of the relative amounts displayed.

3   Bar charts

3.1   Simple bar charts

In a **simple bar chart** the figures we wish to compare are represented by bars. These can either be drawn vertically or horizontally. The height or length of a bar is proportional to the size of the figure being illustrated.

3.2   Example

Suppose we know that production figures of different car companies are as follows.

Firm	Number of cars produced
Ausota	180,000
Vauxsun	145,000
Moruar	165,000
Trihall	160,000
Fortin	170,000

We will draw a vertical bar chart and a horizontal bar chart to illustrate this.

3.3 Solution

Vertical bar chart

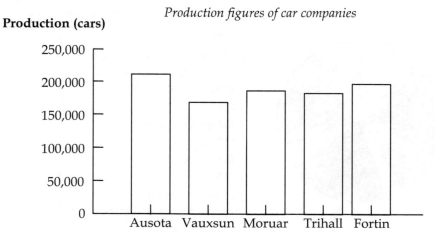

Production figures of car companies

Production (cars)

Horizontal bar chart

Production figures of car companies

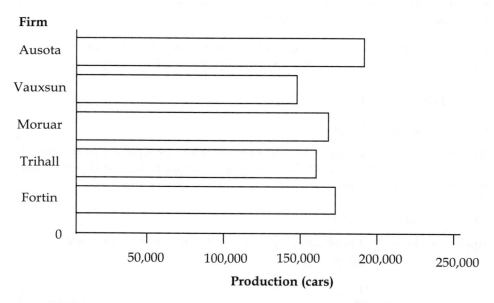

We can put the **appropriate identification** either in the bar itself, immediately adjacent to the bar, or use a key for shadings or colours. There is no need to draw three-dimensional bars; two-dimensional are perfectly adequate and often less confusing. When drawing these charts it is very important to start the scale from zero. A very misleading picture may be shown otherwise.

3.4 Component bar charts

When we draw bar charts the totals we wish to illustrate can often be broken down into **sub-divisions or components**.

3.5 Example

Suppose we have the following table of wine consumption by type and year:

	Consumption figures (10,000 litres)			
	Red	*White*	*Rosé*	*Total*
20X2	59.3	46.5	14.2	120.0
20X3	63.6	47.0	14.4	125.0
20X4	72.3	48.2	14.5	135.0

We will draw a component bar chart to illustrate this.

3.6 Solution

Step 1   Draw a **simple bar chart** of the total figures.

Step 2   The columns or bars are then **split up into the component parts**.

Step 3   Remember to put the key on the diagram otherwise it is useless.

Vertical component bar chart

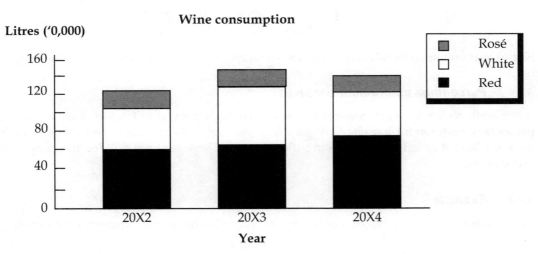

Here, different colours for the different components would be especially effective.

3.7   Example: component bar charts

A shoe firm has three factories. The output of pairs of shoes by factory is:

	20X1	*20X2*	*20X3*	*20X4*
Leicester	350,000	300,000	550,000	400,000
Northampton	200,000	300,000	400,000	500,000
Nottingham	200,000	300,000	300,000	400,000

Draw a suitable diagram to illustrate this information.

3.8   Solution

Shoes produced (000)

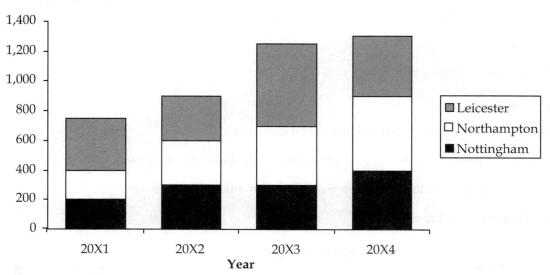

Notice that you **need to calculate cumulative totals** in order to plot these diagrams by hand.

3.9   Percentage component bar chart

If we wish to know what **proportion** of a total each component represents, we can use a **percentage component bar chart** in place of a pie chart. All the columns of the bar chart are the same height or length representing 100 per cent. These are then divided in the appropriate proportions.

3.10   Example

We will draw up a percentage component bar chart for the wine consumption example given earlier.

3.11   Solution

The proportions for the wine consumption example are calculated as:

	Red	*White*	*Rosé*
20X2	$\dfrac{59.3}{120.0} \times 100 = 49.4\%$	$\dfrac{46.5}{120.0} \times 100 = 38.8\%$	$\dfrac{14.2}{120.0} \times 100 = 11.8\%$
20X3	$\dfrac{63.6}{125.0} \times 100 = 50.9\%$	$\dfrac{47.0}{125.0} \times 100 = 37.6\%$	$\dfrac{14.4}{125.0} \times 100 = 11.5\%$
20X4	$\dfrac{72.3}{135.0} \times 100 = 53.6\%$	$\dfrac{48.2}{135.0} \times 100 = 35.7\%$	$\dfrac{14.5}{135.0} \times 100 = 10.7\%$

Percentage component bar chart

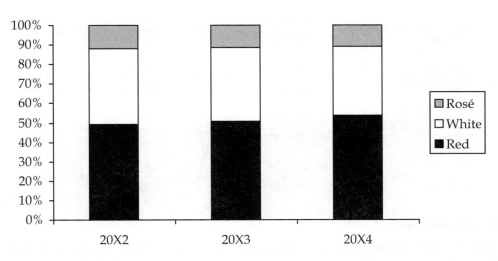

3.12 Example

Draw a percentage component bar chart for the shoe production data.

3.13 Solution

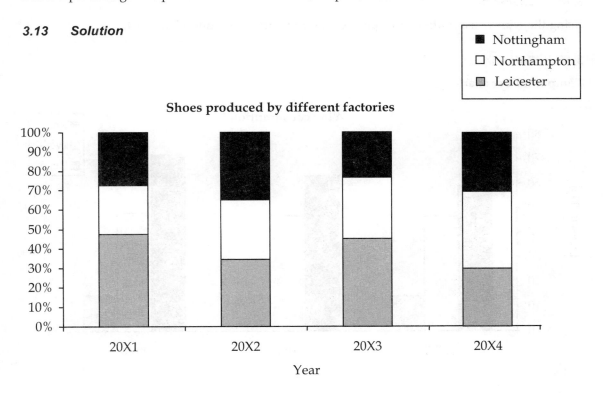

The proportions are worked out using the totals for each year, giving:

	Leicester	*Northampton*	*Nottingham*
20X1	$\dfrac{350,000}{750,000} \times 100 = 46.6\%$	$\dfrac{200,000}{750,000} \times 100 = 26.7\%$	$\dfrac{200,000}{750,000} \times 100 = 26.7\%$
20X2	$\dfrac{300,000}{900,000} \times 100 = 33.3\%$	$\dfrac{300,000}{900,000} \times 100 = 33.3\%$	$\dfrac{300,000}{900,000} \times 100 = 33.3\%$
20X3	$\dfrac{550,000}{1,250,000} \times 100 = 44.0\%$	$\dfrac{400,000}{1,250,000} \times 100 = 32.0\%$	$\dfrac{300,000}{1,250,000} \times 100 = 24.0\%$
20X4	$\dfrac{400,000}{1,300,000} \times 100 = 30.8\%$	$\dfrac{500,000}{1,300,000} \times 100 = 38.4\%$	$\dfrac{400,000}{1,300,000} \times 100 = 30.8\%$

3.14 Compound bar charts

Our concern may not be with proportional comparisons but rather with **comparisons of the component figures themselves.** If this is the case we can use a **compound bar chart**.

3.15 Example

Using the wine consumption example we will draw up a compound bar chart.

3.16 Solution

Compound bar chart

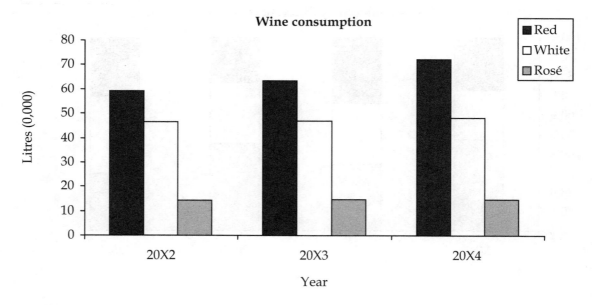

This type of chart allows us to follow **trends of each individual component** as well as make comparisons between the components. It does not, however, give any direct indication of total consumption.

Make sure that you understand the difference between all these different types of bar chart and could produce the one most suitable for the data to be illustrated.

3.17 Example

Draw a compound bar chart for the shoe production data.

3.18 Solution

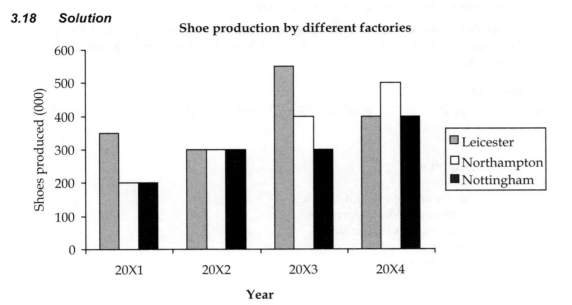

Shoe production by different factories

Activity 2 *(The answer is in the final chapter of this book)*

The table below shows the total UK inland energy consumption, measured in millions of tonnes of coal equivalent, for coal, petroleum and natural gas in the years 20X1 and 20X9.

Energy type	20X1	20X9
Coal	139.3	129.6
Petroleum	151.2	139.0
Natural gas	28.8	71.3

Illustrate this data pictorially using (a) a component bar chart and (b) a compound bar chart. Discuss the benefits of using each method.

4 Rules for drawing charts and diagrams

4.1 Points to consider

When drawing diagrams and charts there are several points to consider:

(a)   Try to make the diagrams **neat** and **uncluttered**. Use a **ruler**.

(b)   If **graph paper** is available, use it.

(c)   The diagram should have a **title**.

(d)   The **variables and scales** should be shown on each **axis**.

(e)   Set the scale so that you use **as much of the paper as you can** for the diagram; this will keep the diagram neater and assist accuracy.

(f)   Units must be indicated on **both axes**.

(g)   Where diagrams are combined or superimposed ensure that each is **recognisable separately** and suitably labelled.

(h)   **Too much detail** on a diagram makes it confusing rather than enlightening.

(i)   Remember the **key** where appropriate.

(j)   Remember to **start scales at *zero* on bar charts**.

(k)   Remember that **component and compound bar charts** become less and less effective the more sub-divisions you use. It is often worth considering **a pie chart as an alternative**.

4.2   Example

In the financial year 20X3/X4 Sheffield City Council had the following major items of expenditure:

	£m
Education	175
Housing	84
Family and community services	41
Policy and general purposes	17
Recreation and amenities	11
Environmental health and cleansing	11
Corporate estate	8

Illustrate this information using a suitable diagram.

4.3   Solution

Adding the figures up, the total expenditure was £347m. Given the number of categories, the clearest form for our illustration will be a pie chart. We must now work out the *proportions* of each category of expenditure and its angle.

	%	*Angle*
Education	$\frac{175}{347} \times 100 = 51$	$\frac{51}{100} \times 360 = 184$
Housing	$\frac{84}{347} \times 100 = 24$	$\frac{24}{100} \times 360 = 86$
Family & community services	$\frac{41}{347} \times 100 = 12$	$\frac{12}{100} \times 360 = 43$
Policy & general purposes	$\frac{17}{347} \times 100 = 5$	$\frac{5}{100} \times 360 = 18$
Recreation & amenities	$\frac{11}{347} \times 100 = 3$	$\frac{3}{100} \times 360 = 11$
Env. health & cleansing	$\frac{11}{347} \times 100 = 3$	$\frac{3}{100} \times 360 = 11$
Corporate estate	$\frac{8}{347} \times 100 = 2$	$\frac{2}{100} \times 360 = 7$
	100	360

The pie chart for the Sheffield City Council items of major expenditure is as follows.

Major expenditure of Sheffield City Council 20X3/X4

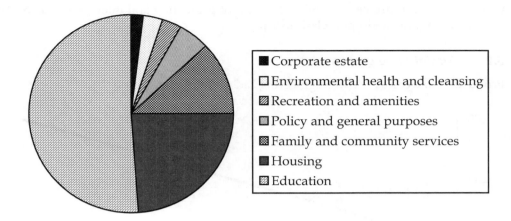

Note: This example is a good illustration of the problem of rounding errors. The % column originally added up to 99 per cent (not 100 per cent) and the angle column to 356° (not 360°), making the illustration only approximate. Education's percentage (50.43 per cent) was rounded up to 51 per cent. The angles were recalculated with these percentages and the problem disappeared.

Activity 3 *(The answer is in the final chapter of this book)*

A computer company has three factories, located in Manchester, Bristol and Derby. The production records of each factory are as follows.

Number of computers produced
(hundreds)

Factory	20X2	20X3	20X4
Manchester	3	5	14
Bristol	11	14	27
Derby	18	26	55
Total	32	45	96

Compare the production at the three factories using component and percentage component bar charts. Comment on these diagrams.

Diagrams such as pictograms, pie charts and bar charts are useful ways of illustrating data. They do not provide precise information but do give users a feel for what has happened.

5 Graphs

5.1 Introduction

Graphs and charts are very useful as a means of presenting and interpreting data. This section introduces **graphs of simple relationships**.

5.2 Straight-line graphs

Production line costs for AM Engineering Ltd – straight line graph

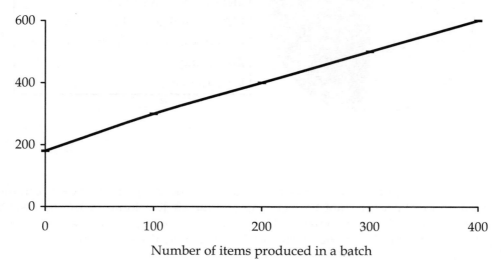

This is a simple **straight-line graph** showing the cost of producing a number of items on a production line. It shows that, even if no items are produced, there is a cost of about £170 to 'set up' the production line. After that, costs increase as production increases at a direct rate.

 This is an example of a graph of a semi-variable cost. There is a fixed cost of £170 followed by a variable element.

5.3 Time series graphs

Sales of Rocco Ice-cream – time series

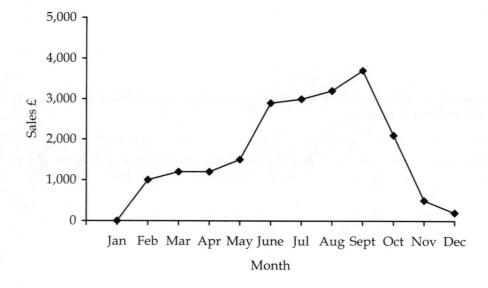

This illustrates the sales of Rocco Ice-cream for the 12 months of a particular year. It shows that, as expected, sales increase over the summer months. The data in such a graph is called a **time series**.

 Time series graphs can be very useful in showing how sales (or other figures) tend to change over a particular time period.

5.4 How to draw a graph

Graphs will have just **two variables, x and y,** which are related. The major points to be remembered when drawing such graphs are given below.

(a) Since there are two variables, two axes are required. The vertical axis is used to represent y, the **dependent variable** in the relationship. The **x variable** is represented on the horizontal axis, this being the **independent variable**.

 You must decide which variable depends on the other. For example, in the production line costs example, the cost of the batch depends on the number of items in the batch, so cost is the dependent variable (y) and number of items is the independent variable (x).

(b) The horizontal and vertical axes are used to represent **both positive and negative values**. This is done by dividing the graph into four quadrants as shown below.

y

x

(c) The point where the axes intersect is called the **origin** and is where x = 0 and y = 0. The four quadrants are used for the following values of x and y.

y

Second quadrant	First quadrant
x negative	x positive
y positive	y positive

Third quadrant	Fourth quadrant
x negative	x positive
y negative	y negative

x

For example, the point x = 2, y = 3 falls in the first quadrant

" x = –2, y = 3 falls in the second quadrant

" x = –2, y = –3 falls in the third quadrant

" x = 2, y = –3 falls in the fourth quadrant

Most graphs that you will draw will only use the first quadrant (x and y both positive)!

(d)   Choosing **suitable scales** for the axes is very important. When using graph paper, the squares are divided up in multiples of ten and it is therefore logical to use multiples of ten for the intervals on the scale. It is not practical to use intervals of, say, three or seven on an axis.

(e)   The **intervals for the scales need not be the same** for both the x and y axes. For example, an interval of five units on the x-axis and 100 units on the y-axis is permissible. Care should, therefore, be taken to examine the scales of the x and y axes when interpreting a graph.

(f)   Always remember to **label the axes** on a graph. The minimum requirement is to label them x and y (or some other letters). If the graph has a practical meaning, then label the axes with the actual title of the variable.

5.5   *Example – graph of a non-linear relationship*

Draw a graph of the following values:

x	5	–10	–5	–2	10	15
y	50	–100	–50	20	75	25

5.6   *Solution*

In this data, the x values range from –10 to +15, while the y values range from –100 to +75. Our scales, logically based on intervals of a multiple of 10, must therefore cover these ranges. It would not be sensible in this example to use the same scale for both the x and y axes because of the very different ranges.

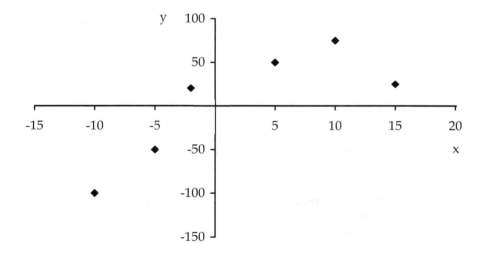

 A graph is a much more accurate method of representing data than most of the diagrams considered earlier. Therefore, it is important that a graph is drawn up accurately.

6   Summary

When asked to extract and provide information for someone in your organisation, it may be enough to simply provide this information in narrative form in a note, a letter, a memo, a report or in an e-mail. However, where there are large amounts of information involved it may be more appropriate to include in the report or memo etc. a table, diagram, bar chart or graph if this makes the information clearer and more easily understood. The important points with all forms of tables, charts or diagrams is to make them neat, to label them clearly and to include only the figures that are relevant and required.

7 *Quick Quiz*

For the following presentation methods, give one relative advantage and one relative disadvantage of the first over the second:

1   Table, pictogram

2   Simple bar chart, pie chart

3   Component bar chart, compound bar chart

CHAPTER 9

Introduction to forecasting (budgeting)

FOCUS

This chapter covers the following Knowledge and Understanding and Performance Criteria of the AAT Standards of Competence:

The purpose of management information: decision making; planning and control *(Knowledge and Understanding element 4.1)*

The role of management information in the organisation *(Knowledge and Understanding element 4.2)*

Compare information extracted from a particular source with actual results *(Performance Criteria element 4.2)*

Identify discrepancies *(Performance Criteria element 4.2)*

Provide comparisons to the appropriate person in the required format *(Performance Criteria element 4.2)*

In order to cover these the following topics are covered:

◆ Forecasting (budgeting)

◆ Standard costing

Key terms	
Forecast	A statement of the future revenues, planned costs and resulting cashflows for a particular period.
Forecast (standard) cost	The planned unit cost of the products, components or services produced in a period.
Discrepancy (variance)	The difference between a standard cost/revenue/profit and the corresponding actual result.

1 Forecasting (budgeting)

1.1 Introduction

 A budget is a predetermined set of costs and income that is calculated before the accounting period starts. It is an estimate of the costs and income for the period.

1.2 Purpose of budgeting

The purpose of budgeting is to help management in the processes of decision making, planning and control.

1.3 Budgeting process

In brief the budgeting process is as follows:

Step 1 Determine the key budget factor

This is the factor that in practice sets the limit to the quantity of production. Usually this will be the estimated number of units of each product that can be sold in the period.

Step 2 Once the number of units of sales have been determined then the production budget can be drawn up. This is the number of units of each product required to be produced in the period.

Step 3 Produce the materials purchases budget based upon the amount of production for the period. This will be in units (eg kilograms of materials).

Step 4 Produce the materials cost budget based upon the units in the materials purchases budget and the estimated price of materials.

Step 5 Produce the labour hours budget based upon the labour needed to produce the necessary units for the period. Convert the labour hours budget to a labour cost budget using estimated labour rates.

Step 6 Produce the other cost budgets, eg, expenses, administration costs, canteen costs etc.

1.4 Master budget

Finally all of these individual budgets are brought together in a master budget which is usually made up of a budgeted profit and loss account for the period and a budgeted balance sheet at the end of the period. There might also be a cash flow budget produced.

1.5 Comparison of budget and actual

As you will see in more detail in the next chapter one of the comparisons that you may need to produce is that of the budgeted figures for the period compared to the actual results of the period.

 Note that for Unit 4 you do not need to produce budgets but you may need to compare budgeted figures to actual figures.

2 Standard costing

2.1 Introduction

Cost accounting is usually carried out on an **historical basis**.

♦   A **budget** is prepared for a period

♦   Costs are accumulated and analysed **after they have been incurred**.

♦   **Comparison of budget and actual cost** is then made some time after the end of the period in question.

This approach suffers from two basic problems:

(a)   any information obtained from the comparison may be **too late to be effective**;

(b)   the cost headings are frequently **too general** to enable management to pinpoint reasons for the differences from budget.

Clearly, management needs a system that provides more **immediate and detailed information as to why budgeted performance differs from actual performance**.

2.2   Standard costing system

Standard costing provides such a system. It gives a set of predetermined benchmarks for factors such as material usage per unit produced against which actual performance can be measured.

A standard cost is a predetermined cost which is calculated from management's standards of efficient operation and the relevant necessary expenditure. It may be used as a basis for fixing selling prices, for valuing stock and work in progress, and to provide control over actual costs through the process of **variance analysis**.

Standard costing is the preparation and use of standard costs, their comparison with actual costs, and the analysis of variances to their causes.

Variances are where actual results differ from the predetermined standards.

 Standard costs are made up of the expected usage of a resource and the expected cost of that resource.

2.3   Types of standard

The way in which control is exercised and the interpretation and use of variances from standards will depend on the **manner in which those standards are set**. There are various different types of standard that can be set.

2.4   Ideal standards

In some cases, standards are established on the assumption that machines and employees will work with **optimal efficiency** at all times and that there will be no stoppages and no loss of materials or services.

Such standards would represent an **ideal state of affairs** and therefore the objectives they set are never achieved.

Managers who are responsible for the costs can hardly approve of targets which they can never reach and which, therefore, result in large adverse variances from the standards.

2.5   Attainable (expected) standards

In other cases, the standards set will be those which are **reasonably attainable**, consideration being given to the state of efficiency which can be achieved from the existing facilities. There is no question of assuming, as for ideal standard costs, that production resources will be used at maximum efficiency.

A **positive effort** is still made to achieve a high level of efficiency, but there is no question of going beyond what is attainable.

2.6 Basic standards

A **basic standard** is one which, having been fixed, is not generally revised with changing conditions, but remains in force for a long period of time. It may be set originally having regard to either ideal or expected conditions. Under circumstances of rapid technological change or of significant price changes, basic standards are of limited value.

 There may be variations on these methods, but the aim should be to select the standard cost which is likely to be **the most realistic for the business concerned**. It should be remembered that standards are the yardstick against which efficiency is measured and if they are unrealistic then the variances will be of little meaning.

2.7 Advantages of standard costing

The advantages of standard costing fall into two broad categories: **planning and control**.

(a) **Planning**

Predetermined standards make the preparation of forecasts and budgets much easier. If the standards are to be used for these operational decisions, then they must obviously be as accurate as possible. This again means that standards should be revised on a frequent basis.

(b) **Control**

Control is exercised (primarily) through the comparison of standard and actual results, and the isolation of variances. This will highlight areas of apparent efficiency and inefficiency, and investigation of the causes of variances can be made as considered necessary. This will enable corrective action to be taken to improve efficiency in the future.

In addition to the above, there are **subsidiary advantages** such as:

(a) If the standards are perceived to be attainable, they will then serve to **motivate the employees** concerned.

(b) A **standard costing bookkeeping system** can be set up that will fulfil all requirements, for both internal and external reporting.

(c) **Recording of stock issues** is simplified, as it is done at the standard price.

2.8 Disadvantages of standard costing

These relate primarily to the **costs incurred in setting up and maintaining the system**. As indicated, standards must be revised on a regular basis to retain their usefulness. It is for this reason that standard costing is most effective for well-established and repetitive processes, so that the revisions of standards are kept to a minimum.

2.9 Example

It is estimated that one unit of a product requires 3 kg of material X and 5 kg of material Y. Material X costs £12 per kilogram and material Y costs £4 per kilogram.

What is the standard material cost of one unit of this product?

2.10 Solution

		£
Material X	3kg @ £12	36
Material Y	5kg @ £4	20
		56

This standard material cost is the estimated cost of the materials for one unit of this product.

Activity 1 *(The answer is in the final chapter of this book)*

The labour cost of a product is being considered. It is estimated that each unit will require 2 hours of grade A labour time and 4 hours of grade C labour time. The labour rates for the next accounting period are:

Grade A   £12 per hour
Grade B   £10 per hour
Grade C   £8.50 per hour

What is the standard labour cost for one unit of this product?

2.11   Variance analysis

We have explained how management will develop standard costs in advance of the period under review. During the period, **actual costs will be compared with standard costs** and any differences isolated for investigation as to their causes. This will enable any corrective action to be taken as soon as possible.

3   Summary

This chapter has introduced you to some of the basic planning and control elements of management accounting, budgeting and standard costing. For Unit 4 you only require an appreciation of the processes for budgeting, standard costing and variance analysis but you may have to use budgets and standard costs to provide the comparisons that are required for the Unit 4 Performance Criteria. This will be considered in more detail in the next chapter.

4   Quick Quiz

1   Give two possible key budget factors that might prevail in a particular period.

2   What information would be needed to formulate the standard labour cost element of a manufactured unit?

3   What is meant by an attainable or expected standard?

4   How does standard costing contribute towards the control function of management?

CHAPTER 10

Comparison of information

FOCUS

This chapter covers the following Knowledge and Understanding and Performance Criteria of the AAT Standards of Competence:

> Methods of presenting information, including word processed documents *(Knowledge and Understanding element 4.2)*

> Handling confidential information *(Knowledge and Understanding element 4.2)*

> Relevant understanding of the organisation's accounting systems and administrative systems and procedures *(Knowledge and Understanding elements 4.1 and 4.2)*

> The organisation's confidentiality requirements *(Knowledge and Understanding element 4.2)*

> Clarify information requirements with the appropriate person *(Performance Criteria element 4.2)*

> Compare information extracted from a particular source with actual results *(Performance Criteria element 4.2)*

> Identify discrepancies *(Performance Criteria element 4.2)*

> Provide comparisons to the appropriate person in the required format *(Performance Criteria element 4.2)*

> Follow organisational requirements for confidentiality strictly *(Performance Criteria element 4.2)*

In order to cover these the following topics are covered:

♦   Extracting information

♦   Previous periods and corresponding periods

♦   Budgeted figures

♦   Confidentiality

Key terms	
Adverse variance	Where actual cost is higher (or actual revenue is lower) than expected (budget).
Favourable variance	Where actual cost is lower (or actual revenue is higher) than expected (budget).
Flexed budget	Costs and revenues in the budget are adjusted proportionately to reflect the actual level of activity (production/sales).

1 Extracting information

1.1 Introduction

For this element of Unit 4 you need to be able to find information regarding a previous period's costs and income, and forecast costs and income, and then to compare these to current actual costs. Therefore it is important that you are able to find all of this information within the organisation's accounting and filing systems.

1.2 Previous period's costs and income

Information regarding the costs and income of previous accounting periods will be filed within the organisation's filing system. Therefore you should become familiar with the system to ensure that you are able to find cost and income figures for earlier months of the current accounting period as well as figures for the previous accounting period.

1.3 Budgeted costs and income

We have seen the process for setting budgets for future accounting periods. These budgets again will be filed and you must ensure that you can find them easily.

1.4 Materials costs

We have seen in an earlier chapter how the details of each type of raw material are kept in the stores record card. The stores record card initially shows the quantities of each material received from suppliers and the quantities of each material issued to the factory floor. We also saw how the accounts department then added the costs of the purchases taken from the purchase invoice.

Therefore when information is required about the current costs of materials used in the accounting period then the stores ledger card for that material is where the information can be found.

1.5 Labour costs

The details of the labour costs for the period can be found from a number of different sources. However, the most likely place to find details of the total labour cost for the period will be the wages expense account.

1.6 Example

The total gross labour cost for the previous week was £154,000. You are given details of how this is made up:

	£
Factory employees	98,000
Sales employees	24,000
Administration employees	32,000

Show how this would appear in the wages expense account.

1.7 Solution

Wages expense account

	£		£
Gross wages cost	154,000	Factory cost – production account	98,000
		Sales cost – selling and distribution costs account	24,000
		Administration cost – administrative costs account	32,000
	154,000		154,000

Note that each individual type of labour cost is being transferred out of the wages expense account to its own relevant cost accounting ledger account. The cost of employees working in the factory appears in the production account as follows:

Production account

	£		£
Labour cost	98,000		

The cost of the sales force appears in the selling and distribution costs account as follows:

Selling and distribution costs account

	£		£
Labour cost	24,000		

This account would also be debited with any expenses incurred by the sales force.

Finally the administration labour costs are debited to an administrative costs account as follows:

Administrative costs account

	£		£
Labour cost	32,000		

Again this account would also be debited with the expenses incurred by the administration cost centre.

 For Unit 4 you do not need to understand the detailed cost bookkeeping records but you may need to use the wages expense account in order to determine the labour cost for a particular cost centre for the period and this is covered in Unit 2.

1.8 Expenses

We saw in an earlier chapter that when expenses were incurred then they were coded in order that they are charged to the correct cost centre. In the previous paragraph the basic elements of the cost bookkeeping system were introduced and we have seen where each cost centre's expenses would be recorded.

Factory expenses – Production account
Selling expenses – Selling and distribution costs account
Administration expenses – Administrative costs account

1.9   Sales

Sales will be recorded in the cost bookkeeping records as a credit in the sales account (remember that income is always a credit entry). As we saw in the chapter considering the sales function it is likely that sales will be analysed by product or by geographical area. Therefore at the coding stage enough detail must be given in order for the sales to be recorded in separate sales accounts for each product or each geographical division.

2   Previous periods and corresponding periods

2.1   Introduction

Usually the accounting period of a year will be split, for management accounting control purposes, into either the twelve months of the year or more likely into the 52 weeks of the year.

A **previous control** period will be an earlier month or week of the current accounting period.

A **corresponding control** period will be a month or week from the previous accounting period.

2.2   Comparison of information

There are many ways in which you might be requested to compare current costs and income to previous and corresponding control periods. In this section some typical examples will be considered.

 It is always important to ensure that you understand precisely what is required of you as this comparison is likely to be a time consuming process and you do not want to waste time extracting information that is not required. Therefore if you have any doubts about precisely what information is required then always check with the appropriate person.

2.3   Example

Your organisation operates its sales function in three divisions, A, B and C and records sales separately for each division. You have been asked to compare this months sales (June) to those of the previous month. You have found the May information from the management accounting filing system and they are as follows:

	£
Division A	113,000
Division B	258,000
Division C	142,000

You have also found the sales ledger accounts for June which are as follows:

Sales account – Division A

	£		£
		Sales June	129,000

Sales account – Division B

	£		£
Sales returns June	15,000	Sales June	250,000

Sales account – Division C

	£		£
		Sales June	120,000

You are required to compare the sales for June to those for the month of May in a suitable manner.

2.4 Solution

Probably the simplest method of comparing this information would be in the form of a table showing the sales for each division and in total for each month. Care should be taken with Division B's sales and the returns must be deducted from the sales figure therefore a net sales balance should be found on that account as follows:

Sales account – Division B

	£		£
Sales returns June	15,000	Sales June	250,000
Balance c/d	235,000		
	250,000		250,000

Now a simple table can be prepared:

Divisional sales for May and June

	May £	June £	Increase/ (decrease) £
Division A	113,000	129,000	16,000
Division B	258,000	235,000	(23,000)
Division C	142,000	120,000	(22,000)
Total	513,000	484,000	(29,000)

It might also be useful to include a further column to show the percentage increase or decrease in sales. The percentage change would be calculated as a percentage of the May sales as follows:

Division A $\quad \dfrac{16,000}{113,000} \times 100 = 14.2\%$

Division B $\quad \dfrac{(23,000)}{258,000} \times 100 = (8.9\%)$

Division C $\quad \dfrac{(22,000)}{142,000} \times 100 = (15.5\%)$

Total $\quad \dfrac{(29,000)}{513,000} \times 100 = (5.7\%)$

The table would then appear as follows:

Divisional sales for May and June

	May £	June £	Increase/ (decrease) £	Increase/ (decrease) %
Division A	113,000	129,000	16,000	14.2
Division B	258,000	235,000	(23,000)	(8.9)
Division C	142,000	120,000	(22,000)	(15.5)
Total	513,000	484,000	(29,000)	(5.7)

This information could also be shown in a compound bar chart as was considered in an earlier chapter. It may also be analysed using spreadsheets as discussed in the next chapter.

Activity 1 *(The answer is in the final chapter of this book)*

You have been asked to compare the month 2 labour cost from last year to the month 2 labour cost for this year.

From the filed management accounts for last year you discover that the month 2 labour cost was broken down as follows:

	£
Production labour cost	336,000
Selling department labour cost	248,000
Administration department labour cost	100,000

The wages expense account for month 2 of this year is as follows:

Wages expense account

	£		£
Gross wages cost	990,000	Work-in-progress account	510,000
		Selling costs account	350,000
		Administration costs account	130,000

You are required to compare the labour costs for month 2 of the current period and the corresponding period.

2.5 Interpreting comparisons

The activity above shows that there have been large increases in labour costs in all areas of the organisation over the last year. Before drawing any conclusions from such a situation it is important to ensure that you are comparing like with like. For example, if production and sales quantities had increased dramatically between month 2 of last year and month 2 this year then this should be recognised in the comparison of costs.

This will now be considered in an extension to this activity.

2.6 Example

Continuing with the activity above suppose that you now discover the following information:

	Previous year Month 2	Current year Month 2
Production in units	100,000	150,000
Sales staff	20	30

It has also been estimated by the administration manager that due to increased production and sales the time spent by personnel on administration has increased by 25%.

You are required to prepare an analysis of the month 2 labour costs taking this additional information into account.

2.7 Solution

Given the significantly different production and sales levels between the two months, it is clear that in the previous activity we were not comparing like with like. What is necessary is to **flex** (adjust proportionately) the previous year's figures to indicate what they would have been if there had been this year's activity levels.

Therefore the previous year's figures would be flexed as follows:

£

Production labour $336,000 \times \dfrac{150,000}{100,000}$ 504,000

Sales labour $248,000 \times 30/20$ 372,000

Administration $100,000 \times 1.25$ 125,000

The revised table would be as follows:

Labour cost – month 2

	Prior year £	Prior year Flexed £	Current year £	Increase/ (decrease) £
Production	336,000	504,000	510,000	6,000
Sales	248,000	372,000	350,000	(22,000)
Administration	100,000	125,000	130,000	5,000
Total	684,000	1,001,000	990,000	(11,000)

This clearly shows a very different picture from the answer to the previous activity and highlights the importance of ensuring that comparisons are valid.

When comparing information it is important to check that you are comparing like with like otherwise the comparison will have little meaning.

3 Budgeted figures

3.1 Introduction

Comparison might also be required between forecast or budgeted figures for a period and the actual results of the period.

3.2 Example

You have been asked to prepare a comparison of the budgeted cost of materials and labour for production in week 17 to the actual cost for the week.

The budgeted costs were found in the filing system and it was discovered that they were as follows:

	£
Material X	117,000
Material Y	330,000
Labour	226,000

The actual costs for the period are as follows:

MATERIAL DESCRIPTION   Material X
Code   M100

Date	Receipts			Issues			Balance		
	Quantity	Unit price £	Total £	Quantity	Unit price £	Total £	Quantity	Unit price £	Total £
Bal b/f							10,000	15.00	150,000
Week 17				8,000	15.00	120,000	2,000	15.00	30,000

MATERIAL DESCRIPTION   Material Y
Code   M101

Date	Receipts			Issues			Balance		
	Quantity	Unit price £	Total £	Quantity	Unit price £	Total £	Quantity	Unit price £	Total £
Bal b/f							130,000	2.50	325,000
Week 17				100,000	2.50	250,000	30,000	2.50	75,000

Wages expense account

	£		£
Gross wages	470,000	Production costs	230,000
		Selling costs	110,000
		Administration costs	130,000

You also determine that the budget was based upon an anticipated production level of 10,000 units whereas actual production was only 8,000 units for the week.

You are required to prepare a comparison of the budgeted and actual figures for week 17.

3.3 Solution

Step 1   **Flex the budget**

Material X $£117,000 \times \dfrac{8,000}{10,000} = £93,600$

Material Y $£330,000 \times \dfrac{8,000}{10,000} = £264,000$

Labour $£226,000 \times \dfrac{8,000}{10,000} = £180,800$

Step 2 Compare actual and flexed costs

Costs – week 17

	Budget year £	Flexed £	Actual £	Variance £
Material X	117,000	93,600	120,000	26,400 adverse
Material Y	330,000	264,000	250,000	14,000 favourable
Labour	226,000	180,800	230,000	49,200 adverse

Note how variances can be either favourable or adverse depending upon whether the actual cost is smaller or larger than the flexed budget cost.

Activity 2 *(The answer is in the final chapter of this book)*

The budgeted costs for expected production of 100,000 units last week are given below:

	£
Labour	45,000
Materials	60,000
Production expenses	17,000

The actual production in the week was only 90,000 units and actual costs were:

	£
Labour	42,000
Materials	52,000
Production expenses	16,000

You are required to compare budgeted costs to actual costs.

4 Confidentiality

4.1 Introduction

As part of the accounting team you will often find that you have access to documents and information about the organisation that other employees do not have. It is extremely important that you are always discreet and strictly follow all the confidentiality guidelines of your organisation.

4.2 Sales information

When dealing with sales invoices and credit customers it is likely that you may come across information regarding customers' credit ratings and financial position. Such information should never be disclosed.

4.3 Materials and expenses

When dealing with materials costs and expense details there may be many confidential areas that you come across, from suppliers details to sales representatives' expense claims.

4.4 Labour costs

Perhaps most importantly, when dealing with labour costs you may become aware of many personal details about employees within the organisation. Such information should always be treated with the greatest degree of confidentiality.

5 Summary

For Element 4.2 you need to be able to extract information, both past and current, from the organisation's records and to compare this information. Comparisons of a variety of information may be required and this chapter has illustrated the main types of comparison.

 It is essential that you realise that when comparing figures you must compare like with like therefore budgets and other totals must be flexed to reflect the actual production or sales activity.

You may also be asked to analyse such data in a spreadsheet, as covered in the next chapter.

6 Quick Quiz

1   The actual sales for August 20X6 for the Northern Division were £250,000. With what might this figure be compared for management purposes? Give three possibilities.

2   Why is it sometimes useful to show percentage changes as well as absolute changes in a comparison statement?

3   Why is it usually necessary to flex costs or revenues before comparison?

CHAPTER 11

Spreadsheets

FOCUS

This chapter covers the following Knowledge and Understanding of the AAT Standards of Competence.

> Methods of analysing information in spreadsheets *(Knowledge and Understanding element 4.2)*

> House style for presentation of different types of documents, including word processed documents *(Knowledge and Understanding element 4.2)*

In order to cover these, the following topics are considered:

- The use of spreadsheets

- Accessing a spreadsheet

- Moving around the spreadsheet

- Entering data

- Improving the spreadsheet's appearance

- Using your spreadsheet

- Word processed documents

- Importing graphics from a spreadsheet package

- Standard templates

- Automatic corrections

- Spell check

Key terms	
Spreadsheet	A computerised table of rows and columns, forming cells into which numbers, text and formulae can be entered.
What if? analysis	The use of spreadsheets in assessing the impact of different input values on revenues, profits etc.

1 Introduction

For those unfamiliar with spreadsheet packages, this chapter will provide the basic introduction needed to feel confident to 'get into' Microsoft Excel and carry out simple information analysis tasks. This package has been chosen because it is the most popular and therefore the most likely to be used in your college or work environment. The editions and programs that you are using may not be the same as those used in this text. In that case, the screens you produce will not be identical to those shown here. However, all spreadsheet packages will perform the basic functions covered in this chapter and access to a different package will not cause too many problems.

 If you are at all unsure, you should read the manual that accompanies your chosen spreadsheet.

2 The use of spreadsheets

2.1 What is a spreadsheet used for?

Much of the data of a company is likely to be held on a number of spreadsheets. They are a convenient way of setting up all sorts of charts, records and tables, including:

♦ profit and loss accounts

♦ sales forecasting

♦ budgeting charts

♦ breakeven point analysis

♦ mortgage payments

♦ stock valuation

♦ exchange rate charts.

 Spreadsheets can be used for anything with a **rows and columns format**.

2.2 Spreadsheets

A spreadsheet is used to manipulate data. You could define it as a table of rows and columns that intersect to form cells. Each row is identified by a number and each column by a letter (or letters). Each cell has a unique identifier formed by a letter (or letters) and a number.

The word **spreadsheet** has its origins in the large sheets of paper used by accountants, over which they spread their figures and calculations in neat rows and columns. The little boxes made by the horizontal and vertical lines have their counterpart in the PC's spreadsheet and are called **cells**.

Into these cells may be entered numbers, text or a formula. A formula normally involves a mathematical calculation on the content of other cells, the result being inserted in the cell containing the formula. These are not visible when you are entering data but reside in the background.

Because most business worksheets are quite large, extending beyond the edge of the computer screen, the screen is in effect a 'window' into the worksheet. Some or all of the spreadsheet can be printed out directly or saved on disk for insertion into reports or other documents using a word processing package.

 The power of spreadsheets is that the data held in any one cell can be made dependent on that held in other cells, so changing a value in one cell can set off a chain reaction of changes through other related cells. This allows 'what-if?' analysis to be quickly and easily carried out – eg 'what if sales are 10% lower than expected?'

2.3   *Graphics*

Spreadsheet packages tend to offer more than just a spreadsheet; in particular they usually include the option to create graphics – charts and diagrams.

'A picture is worth a thousand words' is especially true when it comes to numbers; a spreadsheet is no exception. Since a column of numbers can be difficult to interpret, a graphical representation can help decipher the information. Spreadsheets give you the ability to choose the part of the worksheet that you want to illustrate, and will graph the figures to your specification or represent them in some other graphical form such as a pie chart or bar chart.

3   *Accessing a spreadsheet*

3.1   *Excel*

In the instructions that follow you will be using the Excel for Windows (or similar) package to create a worksheet, make calculations, enter formulae and copy data.

The following should be read and attempted in full if you are unfamiliar with the use of spreadsheets. If you are confident using spreadsheets check through the notes and exercises for any areas you may not have covered previously.

If you do not have access to Excel it will be assumed that you can use a similar package and you should refer to your manual for the basic mouse clicks.

As you are introduced to more commands, the worksheet will provide more information and give you a way to make business forecasts, 'What if?' analysis. When you have completed your report, you will print out a copy to present to your manager.

3.2   *Running the program*

The way to gain access to the spreadsheet package depends upon the type of computer system in use. A **menu** may be available to allow access to the chosen software by entering a single number or letter or by use of a cursor or mouse.

If you are using the spreadsheet at work, you must check first with your supervisor that it is allowed and that you are using the right version of the software.

If you are working in a **Windows** environment, you will access the spreadsheet package using the mouse. Click on the Start button in the bottom left hand corner of the Window. Keeping the mouse button depressed move to highlight the 'Programs' and then to the package that you want to use. Click on the icon.

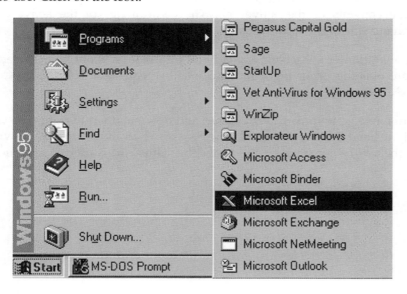

The opening screen in Microsoft Excel might look like this:

(Yours might look a little different if you have a different version of Excel)

On the screen you will see the **title bar**, the **menu bar, the function tool bar** and in the top right corner the buttons to **minimise**, **maximise**/restore and close the worksheet. As with most Windows programs you can change the size and move the Excel Window.

If your screen does not have a formula bar, a formatting bar or a toolbar you can show these by accessing **View** and then Toolbars from the menu at the top of the screen. You can then select (or deselect) what you want to show on the screen. A tick signifies that it is switched on.

The toolbars are below the menu bar. Clicking on any of these buttons provides a shortcut to selecting options from the menu bar. If you pause the pointer over a button a label will appear and, in the **status bar**, Excel will tell you what that button does.

The formula bar is between the spreadsheet and the toolbar. This provides you with information about the contents of the active cell. The co-ordinates of the active cell are displayed on the left-hand side of the formula bar.

The status bar is at the bottom of the screen. It gives you information about your spreadsheet, such as when you are opening or saving a file and whether you have CAPS LOCK, NUM LOCK or SCROLL LOCK on.

Scroll bars are used to move your spreadsheet both up and down and left to right. The vertical scroll bar (on the right hand side of the spreadsheet) is used to move up and down. The horizontal scroll bar (below the spreadsheet and above the status bar) is used to move left and right.

3.3 Vocabulary

The spreadsheet is now ready to go to work, but first you will need to know some basic terms and some spreadsheet vocabulary, so that you can give instructions.

♦ **Worksheet**: a worksheet or spreadsheet (as shown above) is the basis of all the work you do. It could be considered to be the electronic equivalent of an accountant's ledger.

♦ **Workbook**: is a collection of worksheets. The workbook is simply a folder that binds together your worksheets. When you open a new workbook, it automatically contains 16 worksheets.

♦ **Cells**: the worksheet is divided into columns and rows. The intersection of a column and a row is known as a 'cell'. To refer to a particular cell, use its column and row location. This is called a 'cell address', for example A1, B22, etc.

♦ **Columns**: each column is referenced by one or two letters in the column heading. The whole worksheet consists of 256 columns, labelled A through IV.

♦ **Rows**: each row is referenced by the row number shown in the row heading to the left of a row. There are 65,536 rows in Excel.

♦ **Sheet tabs**: these are between the worksheet and the status bar and are used to move between worksheets in your workbook.

♦ **Window**: you can only see part of the worksheet at any time; you could consider the screen to be a window onto the worksheet. You have the facility to move this window, so that you can view any part of the spreadsheet.

♦ **Cell pointer**: look at the cell that is highlighted; this highlighted area is known as the cell pointer. It indicates the cell in which you are currently working. The current cell location is also displayed on the edit line above the spreadsheet.

3.4 Creating and saving a new file

When you first open Excel, a blank spreadsheet appears on the screen and you can start typing straight away. At this point you can work on an established spreadsheet or start on a new one by creating a file as described below.

From the file menu choose the NEW option, and a new Excel workbook will appear on the screen. Once you have created a document, you must save it if you wish to use it in the future. To save a file:

♦ From the **FILE** menu choose the **SAVE AS** option.

♦ A dialogue box will appear.

♦ If necessary, use the DRIVE drop down menu to select the relevant drive; if you are saving to floppy disk, it is generally the 'a:' or 'b:' drive.

♦ In the **FILE NAME** text box type in the name you wish to use (up to 8 characters). All spreadsheet packages automatically add a three-digit extension to your filename. In Lotus it will begin with wk and in Excel it will begin with xl.

♦ Click on the **OK** button.

When you have saved a file once, you do not need to choose the **SAVE AS** option again, but simply choose **SAVE** from the **FILE** menu or click on the icon on the tool bar (picture of a floppy disk).

3.5 Closing a file/Quitting

When you have finished working on a spreadsheet and you have saved it, you will need to close it down. You can do this by either pressing the button at the top right hand side of the worksheet with a cross on it or by choosing the CLOSE or EXIT option from the FILE menu.

If you only want to exit Excel briefly and prefer not to close down the whole package you can switch to another application or back to the Windows Program Manager by pressing <Alt><Tab> repeatedly. This allows you to step through all the opened packages in rotation.

If you have changed the file, Excel will ask if you wish to save the changes you made before closing. Click on the appropriate button.

4 Moving around the spreadsheet

4.1 Cell pointer

The whole worksheet consists of many columns and rows. On opening the spreadsheet, you can only see a small part of it - generally columns A to H and rows 1 to 16. The screen is like a window onto the worksheet and you have the facility to move this window so that you can view any part of the worksheet. The cell pointer highlights the cell you are currently in.

By moving the cell pointer you are able to enter information into any cell of the worksheet. There are a number of ways of moving the cell pointer, but the easiest way is to use the mouse. You can move around the spreadsheet by positioning the **mouse pointer** over the appropriate cell and clicking to select that cell. If the cell address you want is outside the range shown in the current window, it is possible to move down or across the spreadsheet by clicking on the scroll bars to the side or below the Window. Alternatively, you can use the arrow keys on the keyboard.

4.2 Moving directly to a cell: the GOTO command

Sometimes we want to move to a specific address in the spreadsheet that is too far from our present position to warrant using the arrow keys to get there. On the top of the keyboard you can see a row of keys labelled F1 through to F12; these are known as 'function keys'. When these keys are pressed, a special function is invoked. For the moment we will explore the F5 key. This is the **GOTO key** in both Excel and Lotus 123.

Let us assume you wished to go to D19. Press F5 and a dialogue box appears. You are prompted to enter an address or range. Enter D19 and the cell pointer will go directly to cell D19.

Try moving around your worksheet now. You can find where the end is because the spreadsheet will beep whenever you attempt to go beyond the worksheet boundaries.

Activity 1 *(The answer is in the final chapter of this book)*

What is the biggest co-ordinate in your worksheet?

4.3 The help facility

Excel has a comprehensive help facility, which provides both **general** help and **context sensitive** help.

To invoke the help command press the 'Help' button on the menu bar, the ? box on the toolbar or the shortcut key F1. To obtain information on any particular subject shown, move the mouse pointer over the required topic and click, or you may be prompted to type in a question.

Context sensitive help is available either when a help button is displayed in a dialogue box or when an error message is flashed onto the screen. Asking for help at this stage by either clicking on the help button, ? box or by pressing F1 will result in the help window appearing at the topic relevant to the problem encountered.

5   Entering data

5.1   Putting data onto the worksheet

Entering data on the worksheet is very easy. You simply type your entry at the keyboard, press return and whatever you typed will be placed in the current cell, ie where the cell pointer is.

As you type, each character will be displayed on the edit line at the top of the screen. The entry is not put onto the worksheet until you press the return key.

Move to cell A1. Type ABCDEF <Enter>

Now move to Cell A3. Type 123 <Enter>

When you have finished entering data you can either press the <Enter> key on the keyboard or click on the Enter Box (a green tick) on the formula bar.

If you change your mind about entering the data then either press the <Esc> key on the keyboard or click on the Cancel Box (a red cross) on the formula bar.

If you have made a mistake, you can press the 'backspace key' (the key above the ENTER key) to delete what you have done one character at a time. If you have already pressed the ENTER key, you can delete it by highlighting the cell or cells and pressing the Delete key.

There are three types of data that can be entered into your worksheet - text, numbers and formulae.

5.2   Entering text

Text is entered by simply typing into a cell. Typing any letter at the beginning of a cell entry causes it to be accepted as a 'label', rather than a 'value'. If the text you enter is longer than the width of the cell then the text will 'run over' into the next cell. But if the next cell also contains data/information then you will only see part of the text you entered, ie the label will be truncated.

There will be times when you want the spreadsheet to treat a number or a formula as text. To do this you must type an apostrophe in front of the number or formula you are entering, eg '01707 320903 or '=A4+D5.

5.3   Entering numbers

Numbers can be entered on the spreadsheet by simply typing into a cell. If the space in the cell is insufficient, the number will be shown in an exponential form on the spreadsheet, but the number will still be retained in full in the formula bar. If you want to see the contents of cells in full, the columns can be widened to accommodate the number (or text).

 It is not necessary to put the commas in manually when entering large numbers (1,000 or more), because it is easy to format the data to display commas and decimal places to make the data easier to understand.

For example:

◆ Enter 123456 into a cell. Press Enter.

◆ Move the cursor back onto that cell, click on 'Format' in the menu bar, then 'Cells'.

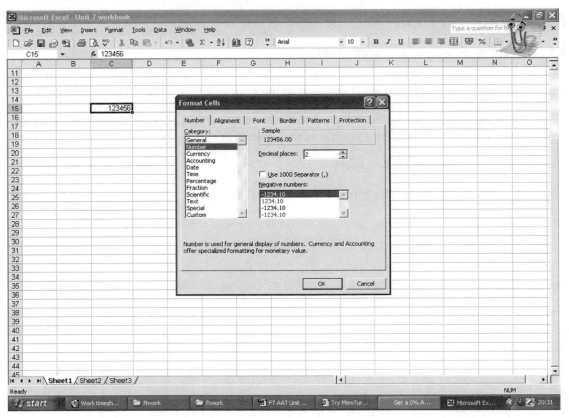

◆ Choose the 'Number' tab and then 'Number' from the category list.

◆ Now reduce the decimal places to '0' by clicking on the down arrow and tick the 'Use 1000 separator' box.

◆ Press OK. Your number should now be shown as 123,456

You can use the 'Currency' option from the category list to put £s in front – try it.

Activity 2 *(The answer is in the final chapter of this book)*

In the previous chapter, we prepared a table manually to compare the results of three sales divisions. You are now required to set up a spreadsheet for this comparison, with the appropriate headed columns and the basic input data, as shown below. In a later activity we shall complete this table by the use of formulae.

Divisional sales for May and June

	May	June	Increase/ decrease	Increase decrease
	£	£	£	%
Division A	113,000	129,000		
Division B	258,000	235,000		
Division C	142,000	120,000		
Total				

5.4   *Entering formulae*

The arithmetic operations and method of writing the basic formulae are very similar in all packages.

 The **BODMAS (Brackets, Of, Division, Multiplication, Addition, Subtraction) rule** must be used to evaluate an arithmetic problem:

♦   Use brackets to clarify the correct order of operation and evaluate expressions within the brackets first.

♦   Calculate "of" expressions (eg 20% of the total).

♦   Perform division and multiplication before addition and subtraction.

♦   Work from left to right if the expression contains only addition and subtraction.

The basic commands for **statistical functions** that operate on lists of values are also very similar throughout the range of spreadsheet packages. Examples of these that you may use for this Unit are:

SUM   The sum of the values in list

AVG   The average of the values in list

A formula always starts with an equal sign (=) in Excel. If you start it with an equal sign (=) in Lotus 123, it automatically converts it to a plus (+) sign. Formulae consist of numbers, cell co-ordinates (eg A2, F7), operators and functions. Operators perform actions on numbers and co-ordinates. Examples of operators are plus, minus, divide and multiply. Functions perform more advanced actions on numbers and co-ordinates.

To enter a formula:

♦   Select the cell where you want to enter the formula.

♦   Press the equal sign (=) on the keyboard (or click on the sign in the formula bar, if one is shown).

♦   Key in the formula directly from the keyboard or use the mouse to select the cells you want in the formula. There are no spaces in a formula.

♦   Press the <Enter> key.

When you have entered a formula, the resulting value appears in that cell. The formula is only visible in the formula bar.

Typical formulae:

=(A6+C10)-E25   Adds A6 with C10 and subtracts E25

=(H19*A7)/3   Multiplies H19 with A7 and divides the total by 3

=SUM(L12:L14)   A quick way of adding L12 + L13 + L14

An even quicker way to add a row or column of numbers is to click the ⌗ button in the toolbar for Lotus 1-2-3. The equivalent button in MS Excel is the Greek symbol sigma. Σ

5.5   *What to do if you make a mistake*

If you enter data incorrectly and you notice the error before pressing the return key then you can use the backspace key, which deletes characters from the entry, working from right to left. For example, let us assume that you wanted to enter the label 'Costs' into cell C1, but instead typed 'Cists'.

♦ Move cell pointer to C1

♦ Type   Cists (do not press the return key)

♦ Press backspace key five times

♦ Type   Costs

♦ Press the return key and 'Costs' will now appear in C1

Another method you can use if you notice the error before pressing **Enter** is to press the **Esc** key. The program will cancel what you have entered and return you to the Ready mode. You then simply re-key.

If you spot the error after you have pressed the **Enter** key then you could simply retype the entry, press **Enter** and the current contents of the cell will be replaced with this entry. For example, if you wished to change the contents of cell C1 from 'Costs' to read 'Total', simply re-key the entry.

♦ Ensure the cell pointer is still at C1
♦ Type   Total
♦ Total will now appear in C1

It would be frustrating if you had completed a long entry, spotted an error, and had to re-key the whole entry again. The spreadsheet comes to your aid with F2 - the **Edit** key.

Move the cell pointer to the cell containing the error, press F2. You will be put into **Edit** mode. The contents of the cell will be displayed on the edit bar with the cursor placed after the last character of the entry.   (Alternatively you can put the cursor at the end of the contents displayed in the edit bar and click.) You may then use the following editing features.

♦ Arrow Left - will move the cursor one character to the left
♦ Arrow Right - will move the cursor one character to the right
♦ Home - will move the cursor to the first character of the entry
♦ End - will move the cursor to the last character of the entry

5.6 Exercise 1 - Basic data entry

In Excel, open a new blank worksheet and enter the following data. Leave plenty of space so that the titles are distinct. You will probably be putting the first invoice number in row 6.

Sales Invoices	August 20X0		
Invoice	Firm	Items	Price
1001	AB Plastics Ltd	10	0.2
1002	J Cables Ltd	21	0.2
1003	DC Covers Ltd	45	0.2
1004	DC Covers Ltd	42	0.2
1005	J Cables Ltd	500	0.2
1006	AB Plastics Ltd	25	0.2
1007	J Hoggs Ltd	300	0.2
1008	L Quick Ltd	1000	0.2
1009	DC Covers Ltd	50	0.2
1010	AB Plastics Ltd	12	0.2
1011	AB Plastics Ltd	15	0.2
1012	J Hoggs Ltd	350	0.2
1013	L Quick Ltd	1500	0.2
1014	J Hoggs Ltd	400	0.2
1015	L Quick Ltd	1250	0.2
1016	DC Covers Ltd	90	0.2
1017	F Browns Ltd	48	0.2
1018	L Quick Ltd	500	0.2
1019	F Browns Ltd	52	0.2
1020	F Browns Ltd	25	0.2

Don't worry if some of the columns don't seem wide enough - type in the whole name – we will adjust this later.

5.7 Adding basic formulae

Excel allows you to build up mathematical formulae to perform many useful functions, eg add up data, find average values, produce variances, add or subtract VAT, etc.

We will look at building up some basic formulae, which are commonly used in financial spreadsheets. In this exercise, we are going to calculate the Net price, the VAT and the Gross. You need to add three more columns after Price and label them: Net, VAT and Gross respectively.

(a) **Multiply** - in the 'Net' column we are going to put a formula to multiply the Items by the Price.

 ♦ Click on first entry in Net column (E6 probably)

 ♦ Type an = in the formula bar

 ♦ Click on first entry in the Items column (or type the address in - C6 probably)

 ♦ Type a * (to multiply)

 ♦ Click on first entry in the Price column (D6 probably)

♦ Press <Return> or OK

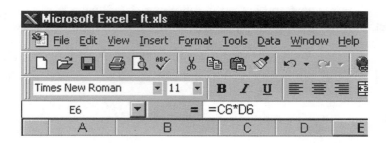

(b) Using the same type of multiply formula in the VAT column (F6 probably), calculate the VAT on the Net figure: this will be =E6*0.175.

(c) **Add** - we want to add the VAT to the Net to give us the Gross figure in G6

♦ Click on G6

♦ Type an = in the formula bar (or click on the = sign)

♦ Click on E6

♦ Type a +

♦ Click on F6

♦ Press <Return> or OK

(d) We have completed the first line of the schedule. Rather than individually repeating these operations for each of the remaining lines, we can simply **copy** the completed line into the remaining lines.

5.8 Copying

Shown below are the Cut, Copy and Paste buttons toolbar at the top of the screen on both Excel (left) and Lotus

 (If you can't see all of these on your toolbar, click on the >> button, which will display more buttons.)

Cut then **paste** is used to **move** cells from one area of the spreadsheet to another.

Copy then **paste** is used to **copy** cells from one area to another.

Copying and pasting or cutting and pasting operations always have two parts:

♦ define the range you want to copy or cut **from**; then
♦ define the range that you want to copy or move **to.**

So, for example, to put in '£' signs across the columns in your sales invoice schedule:

♦ Click on cell D5 and key in '£, press Enter. Go back to D5 and click on the button to place the text in the centre of the cell.

This is the range you want to copy from. (Here the range is a single cell.)

- Click the **copy** button on the toolbar (next to scissors). The border of D5 will start to shimmer.

- Position the cursor over cell D5, hold down the mouse button and drag to the right until cells D5 to G5 have been highlighted (D5 will be white, E5 to G5 will be black or blue). This is the range to copy to.

- Click on the **paste** button on the toolbar. The '£' sign has been copied from D5 and should now appear in E5 to G5.

 You can copy formulae to different cells by the same method. Try to copy the formula from E6 into the range E7 to E25. Then from F6 to F7:F25 and G6 to G7:G25. Note that the cell references change automatically when formulae are copied.

Your spreadsheet should now look like this:

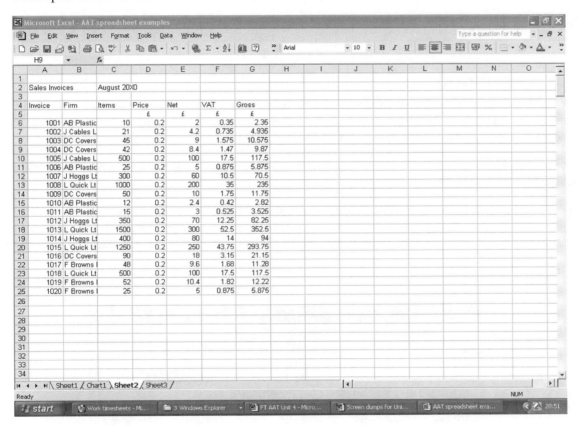

6 Improving the spreadsheet's appearance

6.1 Finishing the spreadsheet

We are going to tidy up the spreadsheet and finish with the totals in row 27.

In E27 we are going to total the column of values in cells E6 to E25.

- In E27 type =SUM(
- Click in E6 and look in the cell value bar. It should now read =SUM(E6
- Type ":" to indicate a range then click on cell E25 and type)
- Press <Return> or OK

The answer to the sum of the cell values should appear in cell E27 (1247). Label this row 'Total' in, say, B27.

All formulae can be entered by a combination of typing and using the pointer.

Note. A shortcut to summary values is to use the Σ symbol from the tool bar.

♦ Try this in columns F and G. In F27 click on Σ and press enter. Excel will automatically total the numbers in the cells above (you should get 218.225 and 1465.225 respectively).

6.2 Formatting numbers

To make your monetary data 100% clearer we need to format it to monetary amounts. For each of the columns with a '£' at the top (probably D, E, F and G):

♦ Highlight the column of figures to be formatted (eg E6 to £27).

♦ Click on 'Format' on the menu bar, then choose 'Cells'.

♦ On the category list choose 'Currency'. It will probably automatically assign a '£' and 2 decimal places. Click OK.

6.3 Formatting text

Making the spreadsheet look good is more than just a cosmetic exercise. Proper formatting, underlining and emboldening can make the spreadsheet easier to follow, draw attention to important figures and reduce the chance of errors.

To format the data you have entered and improve the appearance of the spreadsheet, we are going to do a number of things:

♦ Change the font to Times New Roman throughout. To do this click on the first cell with an entry in it and drag the mouse to the last cell with an entry in it. The area covered should be shaded. Then go to the Format menu and select Cells. Select the Font tab and then the chosen style.

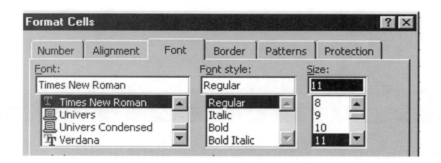

♦ The style format should be Times New Roman throughout with a font size of 14 for the titles and 11 for the main body of the text.

♦ Put the titles in bold. One way of doing this would be to activate the cells by clicking and dragging the cursor over them, then clicking on the **B** button (**Bold**) on the tool bar. Alternatively, all entries in a row or column can be selected by clicking on the letter at the head of the column or the number at the very left of the row.

♦ The Firm column B is not wide enough initially to enter the full details. Change the column width of B to 15 characters by placing the mouse pointer in the column heading at the intersection between column B and C. A two headed arrow should appear. Drag this to the right until the column is wide enough. Adjust the width of the other columns to accommodate the entries comfortably.

♦ Align the column headings. If you look at your spreadsheet so far you will see that all the text is left justified in the cells (moved as far as possible to the left) and the numbers are all right justified (moved to the right in each cell). To adjust this use the align buttons on the formatting toolbar (to the right of the underline U) – say, centre the Invoice numbers, Firm name and Items.

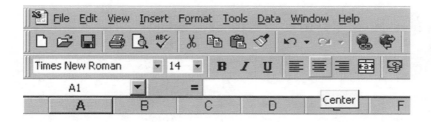

♦ Underline the totals by highlighting the cells containing the totals. Click on 'Format' on the menu bar, then click on 'Cells', then 'Border' tab, and a window similar to the following will appear.

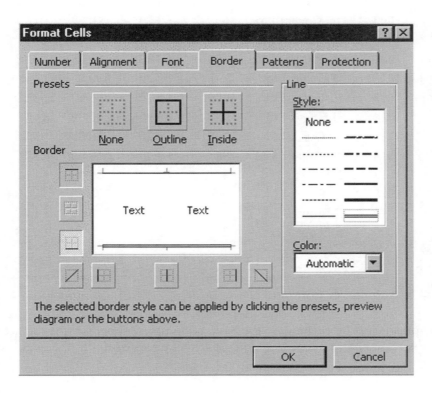

The box on the left shows the edges of the cell or selection of cells, which will have a border. The box on the right shows the types of lines that are available. Click on the top line on the left-hand list and then on the single, non-bold line (probably already selected) in the right hand options. The top of the 'totals' cells should now have a single underlining. Now click on the bottom line and then on the double under-lining style. Click on OK.

The finished spreadsheet should appear as follows:

	A	B	C	D	E	F	G
2	**Sales Invoices**		**August 20X0**				
3							
4	**Invoice**	**Firm**	**Items**	**Price**	**Net**	**VAT**	**Gross**
5				£	£	£	£
6	1001	AB Plastics Ltd	10	£0.20	£2.00	£0.35	£2.35
7	1002	J Cables Ltd	21	£0.20	£4.20	£0.74	£4.94
8	1003	DC Covers Ltd	45	£0.20	£9.00	£1.58	£10.58
9	1004	DC Covers Ltd	42	£0.20	£8.40	£1.47	£9.87
10	1005	J Cables Ltd	500	£0.20	£100.00	£17.50	£117.50
11	1006	AB Plastics Ltd	25	£0.20	£5.00	£0.88	£5.88
12	1007	J Hoggs Ltd	300	£0.20	£60.00	£10.50	£70.50
13	1008	L Quick Ltd	1000	£0.20	£200.00	£35.00	£235.00
14	1009	DC Covers Ltd	50	£0.20	£10.00	£1.75	£11.75
15	1010	AB Plastics Ltd	12	£0.20	£2.40	£0.42	£2.82
16	1011	AB Plastics Ltd	15	£0.20	£3.00	£0.53	£3.53
17	1012	J Hoggs Ltd	350	£0.20	£70.00	£12.25	£82.25
18	1013	L Quick Ltd	1500	£0.20	£300.00	£52.50	£352.50
19	1014	J Hoggs Ltd	400	£0.20	£80.00	£14.00	£94.00
20	1015	L Quick Ltd	1250	£0.20	£250.00	£43.75	£293.75
21	1016	DC Covers Ltd	90	£0.20	£18.00	£3.15	£21.15
22	1017	F Browns Ltd	48	£0.20	£9.60	£1.68	£11.28
23	1018	L Quick Ltd	500	£0.20	£100.00	£17.50	£117.50
24	1019	F Browns Ltd	52	£0.20	£10.40	£1.82	£12.22
25	1020	F Browns Ltd	25	£0.20	£5.00	£0.88	£5.88
26							
27		**Total**			£1,247.00	£218.23	£1,465.23
28							

Save your spreadsheet by clicking on the **Save** button on the toolbar (the picture of the disk). There is no need to enter a name this time, as it will be saved under the name you originally supplied.

Activity 3 *(The answer is in the final chapter of this book)*

Go back to the spreadsheet you set up in Activity 2, for Divisional sales. Use formulae to complete the spreadsheet:

♦ Put in totals for the May and June divisional sales using 'SUM' or the $\sum$ button.

♦ Compute the absolute increase/decrease for each division, and in total, using '-'.

♦ Compute the percentage changes relative to May's sales to one dp.
   (Hint: compute change/May's sales, then use Format-Cell-Number-Percentage)

Finally, tidy up the presentation of your spreadsheet.

---

7   Using your spreadsheet

7.1   What if?

Although the spreadsheet that you have completed is very simple, you still have the basis of a powerful planning and analysis tool. Assumptions and figures can be changed and the spreadsheet will automatically recalculate the results. The main benefit of the spreadsheet is the ability to do 'What if?' experiments.

This allows you to see what happens if, for example, the prices are raised with a subsequent reduction in sales. It can also be used to calculate the overdraft facility required if different variables are changed in a cash flow calculation.

7.2   Changing the variables

In your sales invoices spreadsheet, you are going to change some of the entries.

Activity 4 *(The answer is in the final chapter of this book)*

The price to all customers is going to be raised by 10%, but the organisation assumes that AB Plastics Ltd will use another supplier, so they will lose this business. Would the 10% rise be beneficial to the organisation?

7.3   Charts and graphs

Most spreadsheet packages make it easy to draw charts and graphs from the data in your worksheet. In Excel, the Chart Wizard is the icon that looks like a chart.

7.4   Example

Set up the following simple spreadsheet, showing the forecast sales after the 10% price increase:

Customer	Sales (gross)
	£
DC Covers Ltd	59
F Browns Ltd	32
J Cables Ltd	135
J Hoggs Ltd	271
L Quick Ltd	1,099
	1,596

With the two columns selected, click on the Chart Wizard. Select the type of chart or graph that you prefer and experiment with changing the data labels and percentages.   Two examples are shown below.

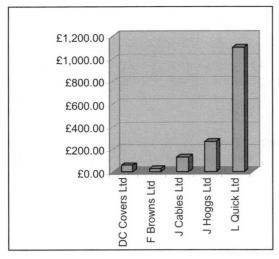

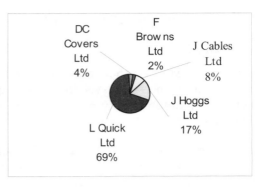

Not all types of graph are suitable for this data, as you will find if you experiment.

7.5 Transferring to another document

Under Windows, you can transfer (or copy) a chart or other diagrams from your worksheet to another document, such as a word processing package. You do this by using the copy and paste facilities.

It is easier if you have both files open at the same time so that you can switch from one to the other using the task bar at the bottom of the screen showing the windows that are currently open. For example, if you are switching from Excel to Word, you just click on the icon with the W on it. Vice versa, it has an X on it.

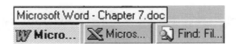

To copy a chart from Excel to a file in Word:

♦ Access the correct area of your worksheet

♦ Highlight the area you want to transfer or copy to another document

♦ Click on Copy

♦ Switch to the other document by clicking onto it on the task bar

♦ Position the cursor where you want the chart to be and click on Paste. You can alter this position by grabbing the picture and dragging it to its position.

Activity 5 *(The answer is in the final chapter of this book)*

Set up a worksheet with the following headings and values:

Sales £m	20X0	20X4	
Cat food	80	120	
Dog food		80	100
Bird seed		25	20

Use your spreadsheet to draw two pie charts showing the percentage make up of the sales for both of the years. Copy both of them to a Word file.

7.6   Printing

To print from your computer make sure that it is connected to a printer and that it is switched on and loaded with the correct paper.

The quickest way to print anything in a Windows environment is to press the **Print** icon on the toolbar. If you want to print more than one copy, specific pages or a highlighted area you must select the Print option from the File menu. If necessary, change the number of copies required or change the page range to specify which pages to print.

To print an area from your worksheet, highlight the area that you want to print. Select **Print Area** then **Print Preview**. This shows you what your print will look like on the page.

The worksheet might be compressed if the page is set up in Portrait. To change to Landscape, click on Page Set Up and change the orientation.

When you are ready to print, click the OK button.

8   Word processed documents

8.1   Introduction

You need to be able to produce a word processed report which will include charts and tables, etc. The purpose of this section is to introduce you to the basic techniques of word processing, and show you how to generate a table in a spreadsheet package (we use Excel).

We are not attempting to provide you with a detailed course on word processing or the use of spreadsheets, that would take far too long and is not necessary for the requirements of the standards. All that is required is that you have reasonable typing skills and can deal with spreadsheets as covered elsewhere in this text.

Note: The following instructions are specifically relevant for *Word 2000*.

In order to illustrate the various changes we can make we are going to use the following sub-paragraph:

99.1   Illustrative paragraph

The quick brown fox jumped over the lazy dog. In order to get more exercise the quick brown fox did it several times. The quick brown fox jumped over the lazy dog. The quick brown fox jumped over the lazy dog. The quick brown fox jumped over the lazy dog. The quick brown fox jumped over the lazy dog.

8.2   Typeface

There are numerous typefaces that are available and any number of typefaces can be used within a document. For example you may want your main headings to be in one typeface with the body text be in another.

There are a number of ways to select a typeface but the easiest keyboard method is [Ctrl + Shift + F], then use your north and south cursor keys to select the typeface that you require. Remember to press [enter] once you have selected the typeface that you require.

Illustration

In order to illustrate this, we shall take the above illustrative paragraph which is currently in Book Antiqua and we shall convert it to Arial.

Step 1

Place the cursor before the first number of the heading of the illustrative paragraph above, hold down the Shift key and use the down arrow to highlight the paragraph.

Step 2

Click your mouse on the small down arrow next to the typeface box on the toolbar. This drops down a menu of typefaces. Use the scroll bar to move up and down the menu and click on the typeface you want (in this case Arial). The paragraph you have selected will now change to Arial.

 You can have great fun converting the paragraph to some fairly extraordinary typefaces, but remember that you are doing this in the context of a business report and funny typefaces are unimpressive, often difficult to read and may well look unprofessional in this context.

8.3 Point size

Again you want may to differentiate text by making text larger or smaller. The method of doing this is similar to that described above, and we shall now illustrate how to convert the same paragraph as before to a 16 point, Arial typeface.

Step 1

Exactly as in step 1 above, highlight the Arial paragraph you produced.

Step 2

Click your mouse on the small down arrow next to the point size on the toolbar. A menu of point sizes will drop down. Click on the point size 16. The paragraph will immediately change to the larger 16 point typeface.

The result of 7.2 and 7.3 above will be to produce a paragraph looking as follows.

99.1 Illustrative paragraph

The quick brown fox jumped over the lazy dog. In order to get more exercise the quick brown fox did it several times. The quick brown fox jumped over the lazy dog. The quick brown fox jumped over the lazy dog. The quick brown fox jumped over the lazy dog.

8.4 Copying text

It is often very useful to be able to copy text from one place in a document to another. This is done as follows.

Step 1

Highlight the text to be copied as described above.

Step 2

Press [Ctrl + C]. Doing this effectively holds the paragraph in the computer's memory but there is no visible sign that anything has happened.

Step 3

Move the cursor to the new location where you want to copy the text and press [Ctrl + V]. The copied text will appear in the new location (and will still be in its original location).

8.5   *Moving text*

It is often very useful to be able to move text from one place in a document to another. This is done as follows.

Step 1

Highlight the text to be moved as described above.

Step 2

Press [Ctrl + X]. Doing this effectively holds the paragraph in the computer's memory and it will disappear from its original location.

Step 3

Move the cursor to the new location where you want to move the text and press [Ctrl + V]. The moved text will appear in the new location (and will no longer be in its original location).

8.6   *Altering margins - 1*

In order to change the appearance of your document, it is useful to be able to alter the margins and alignment of the left hand side of the text. You will notice that in this text book the left hand margin of the text is aligned underneath the first number of each numbered sub-paragraph. You may prefer to align the left hand side of the text with the first word of the numbered title. You may do this as follows.

Step 1

Highlight the text as above (excluding the numbered sub-title).

Step 2

Press [Ctrl + M]. The text of the paragraph will now shift to the right and align the left hand side under the words of the sub-heading as shown below.

99.1   Illustrative paragraph

   The quick brown fox jumped over the lazy dog. In order to get more exercise the quick brown fox did it several times. The quick brown fox jumped over the lazy dog. The quick brown fox jumped over the lazy dog. The quick brown fox jumped over the lazy dog. The quick brown fox jumped over the lazy dog.

In order to return the format of the text to its original, you do the following.

Step 1

Highlight the text to be realigned as above.

Step 2

Press [Ctrl + Shift + M]. The text will move back to the main margin as shown below.

99.1   Illustrative paragraph

The quick brown fox jumped over the lazy dog. In order to get more exercise the quick brown fox did it several times. The quick brown fox jumped over the lazy dog. The quick brown fox jumped over the lazy dog. The quick brown fox jumped over the lazy dog.

8.7 Positioning of text

There are numerous ways that you can alter the alignment of your paragraphs. Below we briefly summarise the ways this can be done. The first step is always to highlight the text. The second step will depend on what effect you are trying to achieve and these are summarised below. We suggest that you experiment with these to become familiar with the sorts of effects you can achieve.

♦ [Ctrl + E] enables you to centralise text.

♦ [Ctrl + J] enables you to justify the text to the left and right. This means that the computer will automatically work out the correct length of each line so that both the left and right margins are perfectly aligned.

♦ [Ctrl + R] enables you to justify text to the right. In this case only the right hand margin is aligned.

♦ [Ctrl + L] enables you to justify text to the left. In this case only the left hand margin is aligned.

♦ [Ctrl + T] enables you to start your text at the left hand margin with all subsequent lines of text aligned to the tab position (this is referred to as a hanging indent).

♦ [Ctrl + Shift + T] returns the second line of text to the main margin.

9 Importing graphics from a spreadsheet package

9.1 Introduction

In the course of producing reports you may frequently want to incorporate graphics (eg charts, diagrams or tables) into the body of your report. The Word package does have some facilities for doing this, but it is more likely that you will want to use the facilities of a spreadsheet to produce many of the graphics that you want. Below we illustrate how this can be done.

9.2 Example

You are writing a report about a drinks manufacturing company and want to illustrate the differences in the consumption of different drinks in the different regions of the country. The information you have is as follows:

	North %	South %	East %	West %
Orange	10	20	30	20
Cola	20	10	20	15
Lemonade	40	20	15	30
Water	30	50	35	35

You want to produce a graphic to demonstrate this in your report. You will do this as follows:

Step 1

Enter the data in the table above into a spreadsheet as described earlier.

Step 2

Decide what sort of chart you want to produce. Highlight the table in the spreadsheet package and click on the appropriate icon on the toolbar. We have decided to use a bar chart which will appear as follows in the Excel spreadsheet. It will be in colour. When viewed in black and white, as in this textbook, it is sometimes difficult to distinguish between the types of shading.

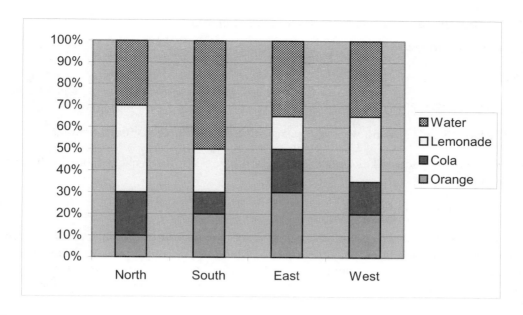

Step 3

In order to import this bar chart from Excel to Word, you have to:

♦ highlight the graphic in the spreadsheet by clicking on the box around the graphic.

♦ press [Ctrl + C].

♦ go back into the Word document you were working in and place the cursor where you want the table to appear.

♦ press [Ctrl + V]. The table will appear in the word document.

10 Standard templates

10.1 Introduction

Microsoft's word processing package *Word* incorporates many features to enable the user to easily generate a wide variety of documents. These are called 'standard templates'.

Every document that is produced is based on a template. A template is a set of formats (page margins, typeface, standard text, styles etc) that is designed for a specific purpose, for example an internal memorandum. Templates are useful because they enable the user to easily produce documents in the same format.

A few examples of standard templates include:

♦ Memos
♦ Reports
♦ Brochures
♦ Letters
♦ Faxes

When a new document is created the user is invited to select one of a number of standard templates as described in the next paragraph.

10.2   *Creating a document with a standard template*

This is done as follows.

Step 1

◆   Click your cursor on 'File' on the toolbar.

◆   Click on 'New'. A window will appear listing the available standard templates.

◆   Click on the required template in the window. We have clicked on the 'professional memo'.

◆   Click on 'OK' in the window.

You will now see the following. As you can see, the standard template you have produced gives you advice on how you are able to modify it. You should experiment with the instructions it gives you. Where it refers to 'styles', you can access the menu of styles by clicking on the small down arrow next to the 'style sheet menu' box on the toolbar (this is the box to the left of the typeface description).

Company Name Here

Memo

To:	[Click **here** and type name]
From:	[Click **here** and type name]
CC:	[Click **here** and type name]
Date:	07/04/04
Re:	[Click **here** and type subject]

How to Use This Memo Template

Select text you would like to replace, and type your memo. Use styles such as Heading 1-3 and Body Text in the Style control on the Formatting toolbar. To save changes to this template for future use, choose Save As from the File menu. In the Save As Type box, choose Document Template. Next time you want to use it, choose New from the File menu, and then double-click your template.

11   *Automatic corrections*

Word contains an automatic correction feature *AutoCorrect* that automatically detects and corrects typographical errors, mis-spelled words, incorrect capitalisation and so on. You may however find that some of the options hinder rather than helps you! An example is where *AutoCorrect* changes (c) to ©.

To display the automatic correction feature press [Alt + T], then press [A].

A window will appear offering numerous alternative autocorrect features. Most of them are fairly obvious and you should experiment in a document especially created for the purpose – not one that contains important information that you would not want to lose.

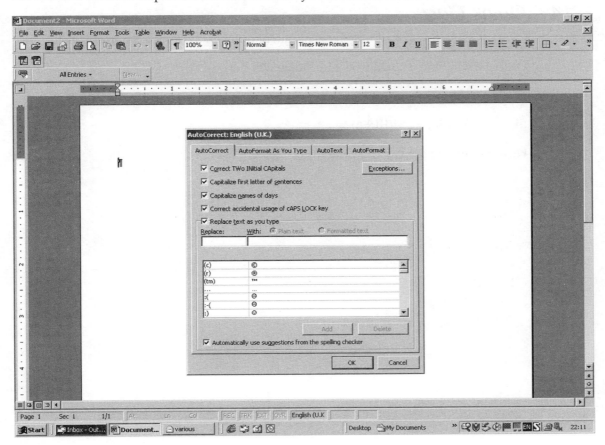

12   *Spell check*

The final Word feature we shall describe is one of the most useful. The spell check feature enables you to check the spelling of all the words in the document you have created. You use it as follows.

Step 1

Move the cursor to the start of the document.

Step 2

Press [F7]. A window will appear containing your document and highlighting the first word that the spell check feature considers to be mis-spelt. It gives you various suggestions on what the word should be, one of which it will have highlighted for you. It gives you various options such as 'change' or 'ignore' and you click on these as appropriate if you want to accept or reject the suggestion.

13   Summary

You started by learning how to enter and exit the software package. Accessing any new software can be a daunting process for the novice, but with practise you will become very proficient in a short time. The main reason for accessing the package is to enter some data and process it somehow to produce the information required. This information should be produced in a format that is acceptable to the person who is to receive it.

You now understand how to improve the appearance of your spreadsheet by formatting individual cells. The examples given are only a few of the many ways in which the appearance of cells can be changed. You should experiment with others on a separate spreadsheet.

14   Quick Quiz

1   Give three methods of adding up a column of numbers on an Excel spreadsheet.

2   Describe what these spreadsheet formulae will do:

   (i)   =(A6+B6)*17.5/100

   (ii)   =F7*F10/SUM(E1:E6)

3   How would you display cell contents of 1234.678 as 1,234.7?

CHAPTER 12

Answers to chapter activities

Chapter 1

Activity 1

Student hours = Cost unit

Computer room and library = Cost centres

Activity 2

D – Pure fixed costs remain exactly the same in total regardless of the activity level.

Quick Quiz

1   Users – internal (management); external (financial).
        Frequency – monthly/quarterly (management); annual (financial).
        Level of detail – high (management); more summarised (financial).

2   Cost centre – central warehouse despatch department.
        Profit centre – a particular sales department in a particular store.
        Investment centre – a particular store.

3   (a)   Fixed

        (b)   Variable

Chapter 2

Activity 1

Task 1

(a)   1120202

(b)   1224204

(c)   1821209

Task 2

A coding system has the following advantages:

(i)   Provides a quick means of referring to individual cost items.

(ii)   Reduces time involved in writing descriptions.

(iii)   Should avoid ambiguity.

(iv)   Should aid data processing, especially input of data.

Note: Only two advantages were required by the activity.

Quick quiz

1   A cost code is a system of letters and numbers which allows cost centres, departments and cost types to be neatly identified and entered into the accounting records accurately.

2   Cost codes enable information to be accurately allocated to the appropriate cost centres.

Cost codes enable information to be collated into appropriate groupings of costs.

Cost codes enable information to be analysed in a variety of different ways by management for reporting purposes.

Chapter 3

Quick quiz

1   A supplier's invoice should be matched against a goods received note before being passed for payment.

2   Goods should only be issued from stores on the basis of a properly authorised stock requisition.

3   With the supplier's code (to update their account) and the goods code (to update the stores records for unit price).

Chapter 4

Activity 1

$$\begin{array}{rcl} & & \textit{Standard} \\ & & \textit{Hours} \\ 50 \times 0.2 & = & 10 \\ 200 \times 0.06 & = & 12 \\ 100 \times 0.1 & = & 10 \\ 10 \times 0.7 & = & \underline{7} \\ & & 39 \times £4 = £156 \text{ earnings} \end{array}$$

Activity 2

(a)   Employee can earn higher wages.
        Employer achieves higher output.

(b)   Difficulty in measuring work
        Need to maintain quality, etc.

Activity 3

(a)   To cost labour to a particular job

(b)   To enable the calculation of wage costs for hourly paid employees

Activity 4

(a)   *Singh*   *Smith*

		£		£
Normal rate	$39^1/2 \times £4.50$	177.75	$41 \times £4$	164.00
Overtime premium	$1^1/2 \div 3 \times £4.50$	2.25	$[(1 \div 3) + (2 \times {}^1/2)] \times £4$	5.33
		180.00		169.33
Bonus	$10{,}500 \times 10\text{p}/100$	10.50	$10{,}900 \times 10\text{p}/100$	10.90
Gross earnings		190.50		180.23

(b)   Gross earnings £190.50 ÷ 10,500 × 100 = £1.81 per 100 sheets.

Quick Quiz

1   To ensure that workers paid on a piecework basis have the security of a fixed amount of income regardless of output.

2   Standard time for 270 units = 324 minutes, actual time = 240 minutes, time saved = 84 minutes.

        Bonus = £6.40 × 50% × 84/60 = £4.48.

3   The basic pay will be analysed between the jobs worked upon as usual. The overtime premiums would be charged to production overhead.

4   A wages analysis sheet or similar document.

Chapter 5

Activity 1

(a) $\dfrac{£3,000 - £200}{4}$ = £700 per annum

(b)   Obsolescence is £(3,000 – 2,100) = £900. This should be written off to the cost profit and loss account.

Quick Quiz

1   The purchase of stock is revenue expenditure.

2   42% × (£2,100 × (100-42)%) = £512 (*note that the residual value is not deducted from the cost – the rate will have been calculated to reduce the book value down to the residual value after three years*).

Chapter 6

Activity 1

	£
Sales (net of VAT) £550,000 × 100/117.5	468,085
Manufacturing cost of goods sold 110,000 × £3	(330,000)
	138,085
Salesmens' salaries	(43,200)
Salesmens' commission	(3,100)
Salesmens' expenses	(5,800)
Head office sales team wages	(21,600)
Head office sales team expenses	(6,700)
Profit	57,685

Quick Quiz

1   Professional organisations, such as solicitors and accountants, will mainly generate new sales through word of mouth. They do not tend to take orders as such – potential new customers will be put in contact with a partner or manager who will talk to them about their requirements.

2   The information required by accounts, stores etc for a new order will be standardised, with internal product codes and the latest prices. These may not be given accurately on the customer's order. In addition, internal orders will be numbered consecutively to help control.

3   The aim is to measure the performance of the sales department – including actual costs of goods/services sold will result in a profit figure that will reflect the performances of both the sales and production departments.

Chapter 7

Activity 1

(a)   Letter

(b)   Short report

(c)   Formal report

(d)   Memo

Quick Quiz

1   To communication information.

2   *Four of:*

         Title page
         Summary
         Table of contacts
         Introduction
         Main text
         Conclusions
         Recommendations
         Appendices
         Acknowledgements
         References

Chapter 8

Activity 1

Bunny and Hutch Ltd
Employees – 20X4

	Number of employees 1 Jan	31 Dec	Average weekly wage £	Total annual wage bill £
Men	2,088	2,124	121.32	12,774,996
Women	1,871	1,860	87.93	8,201,671
	3,959	3,984	105.64	20,976,667

Workings

Number of women employed at 31 December	=	3,984 – 2,124 = 1,860
Number of men employed at 1 January	=	2,124 – 221 + 185 = 2,088
Number of women employed at 1 January	=	1,860 – 97 + 108 = 1,871
Total number employed at 1 January	=	2,088 + 1,871 = 3,959
Average number of men in year	=	(2,088 + 2,124) ÷ 2 = 2,106
Average number of women in year	=	(1,871 + 1,860) ÷ 2 = 1,865.5
Total annual wage bill for men	=	2,106 × £121.32 × 50 = £12,774,996
Total annual wage bill for women	=	1,865.5 × £87.93 × 50 = £8,201,671
Total annual wage bill	=	£12,774,996 + £8,201,671 = £20,976,667

These estimates of the annual wage bill can be obtained in other ways. We could alternatively have used the 1 January figures of number employed or 31 December figures.

To calculate the total average weekly wage we could simply add £121.32 to £87.93 and divide by two. However, this assumes an equal number of men and women employees. Alternatively, since we now have an estimate of the total wage bill, the average weekly wage can be calculated as:

$$\frac{£20,976,667}{3,971\frac{1}{2} \times 50} = £105.64$$

Activity 2

(a)   We first need to calculate the total energy consumption for each year (in millions of tonnes of coal equivalent).

20X1 Total consumption = 139.3 + 151.2 + 28.8 = 319.3
20X9 Total consumption = 129.6 + 139.0 + 71.3 = 339.9

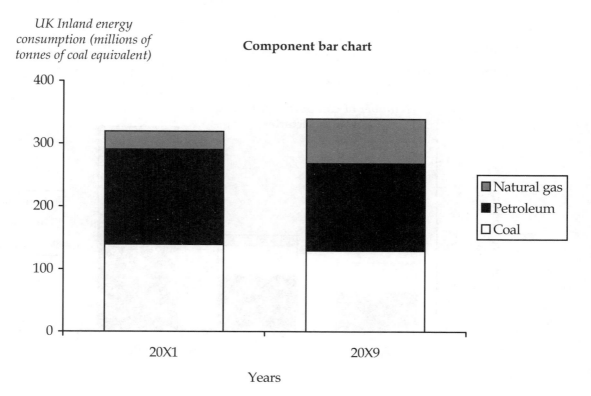

(b)   Compound bar chart

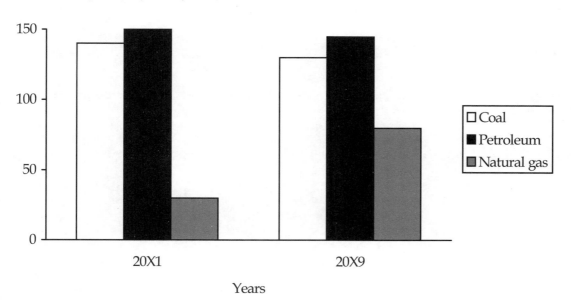

The benefits of the diagrams are:

(1)   (a) shows total energy consumption for each year but (b) does not.

(2)   (b) allows us to use a larger vertical scale than (a), giving increased accuracy.

(3)   (b) shows the trend or change between the years for each energy product. [(a) also shows this trend but not as clearly.]

Activity 3

Component bar chart

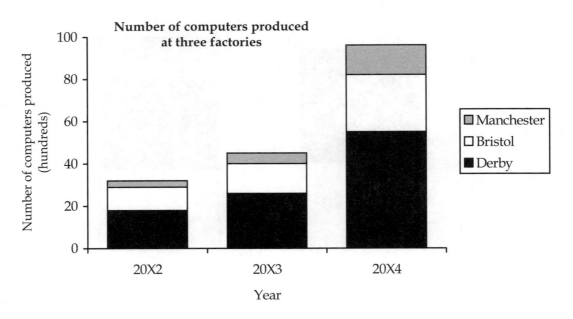

Percentage component bar chart

Changing the data to *percentages* gives:

Factory	20X2	20X3	20X4
Manchester	$\frac{3}{32} \times 100 = 9.4$	$\frac{5}{45} \times 100 = 11.1$	$\frac{14}{96} \times 100 = 14.6$
Bristol	$\frac{11}{32} \times 100 = 34.4$	$\frac{14}{45} \times 100 = 31.1$	$\frac{27}{96} \times 100 = 28.1$
Derby	$\frac{18}{32} \times 100 = 56.2$	$\frac{26}{45} \times 100 = 57.8$	$\frac{55}{96} \times 100 = 57.3$

**Percentage breakdown of computer
production at three factories**

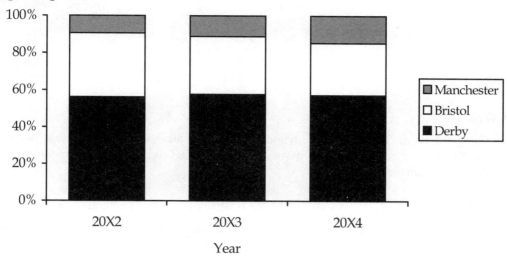

The component bar chart shows that:

♦ total production has increased year by year;

♦ production at the three factories has increased year by year;

♦ production was greatest at Derby, second highest at Bristol and smallest at Manchester in each of the three years.

The percentage component bar chart shows that Manchester has been producing an increasing proportion of total production, whilst Bristol's proportionate production has declined. Derby's proportionate production stayed about the same for each of the three years.

Quick Quiz

		Advantage	*Disadvantage*
1	Table, pictogram	More accurate data	Less visual impact
2	Simple bar chart, pie chart	Can read off total values	Relative comparison not so clear
3	Component, compound bar chart	Shows category totals	Difficult to compare sub-categories

Chapter 9

Activity 1

		£
2 hours @ £12 (Grade A)		24.00
4 hours @ £8.50 (Grade C)		34.00
		58.00

Quick Quiz

1   *Two from:* Sales demand; scarce resource (where availability is restricted to below that required to meet maximum demand – eg skilled labour, a particular material); machinery capacity; cash.

2   Expected productive labour time per unit; expected wage rate(s).

3   A standard that incorporates realistic, if challenging, levels of efficiency and wastage etc.

4   Standard costing helps in control by providing a benchmark against which to compare actual results, thus highlighting any areas of apparent efficiency/inefficiency.

Chapter 10

Activity 1

Labour cost – month 2

	Prior year £	Current year £	Increase/ (decrease) £
Production	336,000	510,000	174,000
Sales	248,000	350,000	102,000
Administration	100,000	130,000	30,000
Total	684,000	990,000	306,000

Activity 2

Flex the budgeted figures

Labour £45,000 $\times \dfrac{90,000}{100,000}$ = £40,500

Materials £60,000 $\times \dfrac{90,000}{100,000}$ = £54,000

Expenses £17,000 $\times \dfrac{90,000}{100,000}$ = £15,300

Compare flexed budget to actual.

	Budgeted £	Flexed £	Actual £	Variance £
Labour	45,000	40,500	42,000	1,500 adverse
Material	60,000	54,000	52,000	2,000 favourable
Expenses	17,000	15,300	16,000	700 adverse

Quick Quiz

1 Budgeted August 20X6 sales for Northern Division

   Actual August 20X6 sales for Southern Division

   Actual August 20X5 sales for Northern Division

2 If the comparison is between, for example, sales volumes of two divisions of significantly different sizes an absolute comparison can be misleading – the larger division may have the largest absolute increase in sales volume, but this may only represent growth of, say, 1% compared to the 10% growth exhibited by the smaller division.

3 One of the main causes of changes in total cost or revenues will be the level of activity – producing twice as many units in a period than budgeted, or than the corresponding period last year, will inevitably lead to a significant increase in total costs. In order to highlight other causes of differences, the two figures must be put on a comparable basis in terms of activity level.

Chapter 11

Activity 1

In the Excel worksheet that is used in this chapter it is IV65536.

Activity 2

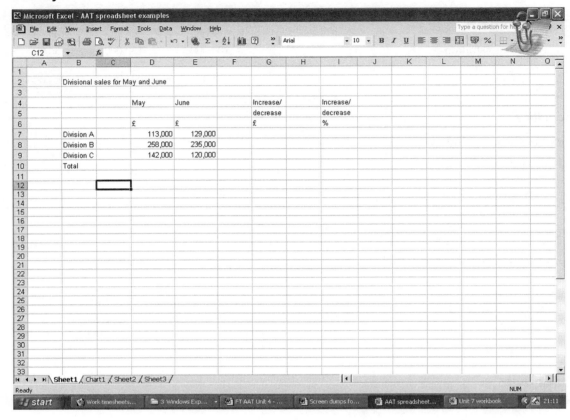

Activity 3

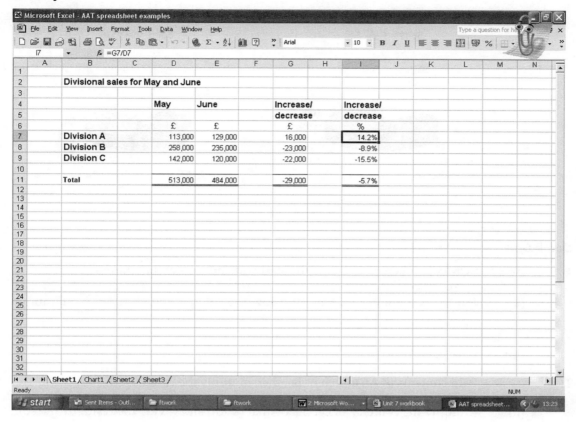

The formulae used were:

In D11: =SUM(D7:D9)   In E11   =SUM(E7:E9)

In G7:   = E7-D7   In G8:   = E8-D8   In G9:   E9-D9   In G11:   = E11-D11

In I7:   G7/E7   In I8:   G8/E8   In I9:   G9/E9   (all formatted to %age)

Activity 4

To do this you should make a copy of your spreadsheet so that you can experiment with it without losing the original information. Highlight the worksheet and go to the Edit menu and select **Copy**. Click on another area of the spreadsheet and press the return key or go to the Edit menu and choose **Paste**.

In the copy version, remove all entries for AB Plastics Ltd and raise the price from 20 pence to 22 pence. The total would now be £1,595.72, which would be more than previously and therefore would be beneficial to the organisation.

Activity 5

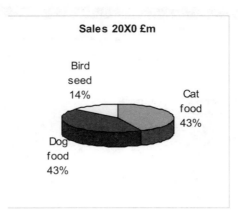

Quick Quiz

1 (i) SUM(x:y) where x and y are the start and end cells of the column

   (ii) Put the cell pointer on the cell below the column and click on $\sum$ button in the tool bar.

   (iii) A1+A2+A3 .....

2 (i) Add contents of A6 to that of B6, then multiply the result by 17.5%.

   (ii) Multiply the contents of cell F7 by that of F10 and divide the result by the sum of the column cells E1 to E6.

3 On the menu bar, click on Format, then on the Number tab, then on Number in the Category list, then select one decimal place and tick the 'Use 1000 separator' box. Click on OK.

WORKBOOK

KEY
TECHNIQUES

QUESTION BANK

KEY TECHNIQUES - QUESTIONS

Principles of cost accounting (covering Chapters 1 and 2)

Question 1

Classify each of the following costs according to their behaviour:

(i)   Monthly rental for the factory;

(ii)   Purchase of materials;

(iii)   Payment of hourly paid employees' wages;

(iv)   Payment of monthly administration staff salaries.

Question 2

A business has a coding system which codes costs with a six digit code.

The first two digits denote the cost centre that the cost relates to:

01   Factory

02   Sales department

03   Administration department

The second two digits denote the type of cost:

04   Materials

05   Labour

06   Expenses

The third pair of digits describe the detail of the cost:

Materials	-	type A	11
	-	type B	12
Labour	-	grade I	21
	-	grade II	22
Expenses	-	rent	31
	-	heat and light	32
	-	office costs	33
	-	other	34

For example the purchase of Type A materials for the factory would be coded as 010411.

You are required to code each of the following costs:

(i)   Factory rent;

(ii)   Administration salaries – grade I;

(iii)   Materials for the factory – type B;

(iv)   Electricity for the administration department;

(v)   Sales representatives' salaries – grade II;

(vi)   Computer disks for the sales department.

Materials and labour costs (covering Chapters 3 and 4)

Question 3

Given below are the transactions for a material, ZZ410, for the month of May 20X1.

Purchases received

3 May	200 units
10 May	180 units
20 May	240 units
26 May	200 units

Returns to suppliers

12 May	40 units

Issues to the factory

5 May	160 units
11 May	180 units
21 May	200 units
30 May	220 units

Returns from the factory

23 May	30 units

You are required to write up the stores record card for the month. There were 30 units of the product in stock on 1 May 20X1.

Stores record card									
MATERIAL DESCRIPTION Code									
Date	Receipts			Issues			Balance		
	Quantity			Quantity			Quantity		

Question 4

A business pays its manufacturing employees on a piecework basis with a guaranteed minimum weekly payment of £285.00. The piecework rates are £2.25 for the first 100 units manufactured in the week, £2.40 per unit for the next 50 units and £2.60 per unit for any further units.

You are required to determine the labour cost for each of the following employees:

(i)   Fred Turner made 160 units in the week;

(ii)   Jenny Smith made 140 units in the week;

(iii)   Karen Allen made 120 units in the week.

Question 5

A business pays its factory workers at an hourly rate of £6.20 for a basic week of 38 hours. Any overtime is paid at time and a half.

For each of the following employees calculate the total gross pay and the overtime premium included in this gross pay.

(i)   George Sellers worked 40 hours in the week.

(ii)   Tracy Tunns worked 46 hours in the week.

(iii)   Jill Sanders worked 43 hours in the week.

Expenses and sales (covering Chapters 5 and 6)

Question 6

A business depreciates its plant and machinery on the straight line basis at the rate of 20% per annum and its motor vehicles on the reducing balance basis at 20% per annum.

At 31 December 20X0 the following figures are available for the plant and machinery and motor vehicles:

Plant and machinery

Cost   £15,200

Net book value   £8,300

Motor vehicles

Cost   £24,200

Net book value   £16,500

You are required to calculate the depreciation expense for plant and machinery and motor vehicles for the year ended 31 December 20X0.

Scenario Based Question 7

Harris Ltd specialises in the manufacture of film storage containers and has two production departments: machining and assembly (in addition to a number of service departments).

From the Goods Received Notes and Material Requisition Slips provided, complete the Stores Record Cards to record quantities received and issued for all transactions. You are not given any information regarding the cost of materials so do not enter anything in the 'unit price' or 'amount' columns.

GOODS RECEIVED NOTE   Warehouse copy

Date: Dec 2   **Time**: 10.35   **No**: 101

Order No: 7124

Supplier's advice note no: 71245

Quantity	Cat No	Description
96	3264	Frame
		Stock code

RECEIVED IN GOOD CONDITION: BS   (Initials)

GOODS RECEIVED NOTE

Warehouse copy

Date: Dec 4   **Time**: 14.50   **No**: 102

Order No: 7022

Supplier's advice note no: 2912

Quantity	Cat No	Description
96	1638	Frame
		Stock code

RECEIVED IN GOOD CONDITION: BS   (Initials)

GOODS RECEIVED NOTE

Warehouse copy

Date: Dec 6   **Time**: 9.30   **No**: 103

Order No: 7125

Supplier's advice note no: 71321

Quantity	Cat No	Description
72	3264	Frame
		Stock code

RECEIVED IN GOOD CONDITION: BS   (Initials)

GOODS RECEIVED NOTE

Warehouse copy

Date: Dec 6   **Time**: 11.15   **No**: 104

Order No: 7129

Supplier's advice note no: 2110

Quantity	Cat No	Description
96	1638	Frame
		Stock code

RECEIVED IN GOOD CONDITION: BS   (Initials)

GOODS RECEIVED NOTE   Warehouse copy

Date: Dec 7   **Time**: 2.15   **No**: 105

Order No: 6041

Supplier's advice note no: 817

Quantity	Cat No	Description
600	364	Dividers
		Stock code

RECEIVED IN GOOD CONDITION: BS   (Initials)

GOODS RECEIVED NOTE   Warehouse copy

Date: Dec 7   **Time**: 3.40   **No**: 106

Order No: 6168

Supplier's advice note no: 015213

Quantity	Cat No	Description
24	3264	Frame
		Stock code

RECEIVED IN GOOD CONDITION: BS   (Initials)

GOODS RECEIVED NOTE   Warehouse copy

Date: Dec 8   **Time**: 9.15   **No**: 107

Order No: 6190

Supplier's advice note no: 2461

Quantity	Cat No	Description
96	1638	Frame
		Stock code

RECEIVED IN GOOD CONDITION: BS   (Initials)

GOODS RECEIVED NOTE   Warehouse copy

Date: Dec 10   **Time**: 10.20   **No**: 108

Order No: 6131

Supplier's advice note no: 890

Quantity	Cat No	Description
600	364	Dividers
		Stock code

RECEIVED IN GOOD CONDITION: BS   (Initials)

MATERIALS REQUISITION

Material required for: 5946   **No**: 1

(Job or overhead account)

Department: Machine Shop   **Date**: Dec 4

Quantity	Description	Code No	Weight	Rate	£	Notes
240	Dividers	364				

Foreman: ×

MATERIALS REQUISITION

Material required for: 5941   **No**: 2

(Job or overhead account)

Department: Machine Shop   **Date**: Dec 4

Quantity	Description	Code No	Weight	Rate	£	Notes
48	Frame	3264				

Foreman: ×

MATERIALS REQUISITION

Material required for: 5941   **No**: 3

      (Job or overhead account)

Department: Assembly Dept   **Date**: Dec 6

Quantity	Description	Code No	Weight	Rate	£	Notes
96	Dividers	364				

Foreman: ×

MATERIALS REQUISITION

Material required for: 5947   **No**: 4

      (Job or overhead account)

Department: Assembly Dept   **Date**: Dec 7

Quantity	Description	Code No	Weight	Rate	£	Notes
12	Dividers	364				

Foreman: ×

MATERIALS REQUISITION

Material required for: 5942   **No**: 5

      (Job or overhead account)

Department: Machine   **Date**: Dec 7

Quantity	Description	Code No	Weight	Rate	£	Notes
120	Frame	1638				

Foreman: ×

MATERIALS REQUISITION

Material required for: 5945

(Job or overhead account)

No: 6

Department: Machine Shop

Date: Dec 8

Quantity	Description	Code No	Weight	Rate	£	Notes
96	Frame	3264				

Foreman: ✗

MATERIALS REQUISITION

Material required for: 5945

(Job or overhead account)

No: 7

Department: Assembly

Date: Dec 8

Quantity	Description	Code No	Weight	Rate	£	Notes
192	Dividers	364				

Foreman: ✗

MATERIALS REQUISITION

Material required for: 5948

(Job or overhead account)

No: 8

Department: Machine Shop

Date: Dec 9

Quantity	Description	Code No	Weight	Rate	£	Notes
120	Frame	1638				

Foreman: ✗

MATERIALS REQUISITION

Material required for: 5950   **No**: 9

(Job or overhead account)

Department: Machine   **Date**: Dec 9

Quantity	Description	Code No	Weight	Rate	£	*Notes*
288	Dividers	364				

Foreman: ✕

MATERIALS REQUISITION

Material required for: 5953   **No**: 10

(Job or overhead account)

Department: Machine Shop   **Date**: Dec 9

Quantity	Description	Code No	Weight	Rate	£	*Notes*
24	Frame	3264				

Foreman: ✕

MATERIALS REQUISITION

Material required for: 5951   **No**: 11

(Job or overhead account)

Department: Machine   **Date**: Dec 9

Quantity	Description	Code No	Weight	Rate	£	*Notes*
24	Frame	1638				

Foreman: ✕

MATERIALS REQUISITION

Material required for: 5948

(Job or overhead account)

No: 12

Department: Machine Shop

Date: Dec 10

Quantity	Description	Code No	Weight	Rate	£	*Notes*
24	Frame	3264				

Foreman: ✕

STORES RECORD CARD

Material: Frame .... Code: 3264

Supplier: T Mayer Ltd ....

Date	RECEIPTS				ISSUES				STOCK		
	GRN No	Quantity	Unit price £	Amount £	Stores Req No	Quantity	Unit price £	Amount £	Quantity	Unit price £	Amount £
Dec 1									24		

STORES RECORD CARD

Material: Frame .... Code: 1638

Supplier: ABT Ltd ....

Date	RECEIPTS				ISSUES				STOCK		
	GRN No	Quantity	Unit price £	Amount £	Stores Req No	Quantity	Unit price £	Amount £	Quantity	Unit price £	Amount £
Dec 1									72		

STORES RECORD CARD

Material: Divider.. Code: 364

Supplier: Shine Ltd...

Date	RECEIPTS				ISSUES				STOCK		
	GRN No	Quantity	Unit price £	Amount £	Stores Req No	Quantity	Unit price £	Amount £	Quantity	Unit price £	Amount £
Dec 1									480		

Question 8

The sales department of a business is run as a profit centre, and for the month of May 20X1 sales of £568,000 were made. The goods that were sold were transferred from the factory at a cost of £390,000. The sales force's wages for the month were £88,000, their expenses totalled £6,000 and their commission was £24,000. The department also spent £18,000 on advertising.

What was the profit made by the sales profit centre for the month of May 20X1?

Methods of reporting and presenting information (covering Chapters 7 and 8)

Question 9

What is the most appropriate method of reporting the following information that has been requested from you:

(i)   the new production manager has asked for the overtime rates for each of the different grades of labour that work in the factory;

(ii)   the board of directors have requested a summary of the cost variances for each of the cost centres and possible reasons for these variances;

(iii)   the purchasing manager has requested from you details of the prices from four different suppliers for a new material that is to be purchased;

(iv)   a customer has requested confirmation of the detailed terms of trade of your business including credit terms, trade and settlement discounts.

Question 10

A business made sales of £49,950 for the quarter January to March 20X1. These were made up of sales of £15,600 in January, £17,100 in February and the remainder in March. Sales for the same quarter in 20X0 were £16,200 in January, £16,800 in February and £16,000 in March. The sales figures for the months of October, November and December 20X0 were £17,200, £18,400 and £17,500 respectively.

You are required to draw up a table showing the sales for this quarter, the previous quarter and the corresponding quarter.

Question 11

The monthly sales figures for a business for the year ended 31 March 20X1 were as follows:

Apr	May	June	July	Aug	Sept	Oct	Nov	Dec	Jan	Feb	Mar
£	£	£	£	£	£	£	£	£	£	£	£
14,300	15,200	14,800	14,200	16,000	15,500	14,900	15,400	14,500	14,000	14,600	14,200

You are required to draw a graph showing these monthly sales figures for the year.

Question 12

Task 1

The sales, total cost and profit figures for Paper Products Limited over the last five years were as follows.

	20X4	20X5	20X6	20X7	20X8
	£m	£m	£m	£m	£m
Sales	6.00	6.40	6.58	7.40	7.10
Total cost	4.20	4.65	5.05	5.80	5.77
Profit	1.80	1.75	1.53	1.60	1.33

Prepare a line graph, using the graph paper on the following page, showing the trend in the sales and profit figures from 20X4 to 20X8 from the data above.

Notes:

1   A bar chart will not be acceptable.

2   One sheet of graph paper is sufficient for this task.

Task 2

The management accountant is concerned that profits have been falling from 20X4 to 20X8.

Prepare notes for a telephone conversation with the management accountant using the notepad given.

The notes should:

◆   outline the extent to which profits have fallen between 20X4 and 20X8;

◆   give reasons for the fall in profits using the data above.

NOTEPAD

Budgeting, standard costing and information comparison (covering Chapters 9 and 10)

Question 13

A batch of production of a product should have used 2,600 kg of material at a cost of £3.40 per kg. Instead the batch of production used 2,700 kg of the material at a cost of £3.40 per kg.

What is the total variance for materials costs for this batch?

Question 14

The costs of production of a business for the months of April 20X1 and April 20X0 are given below:

	April 20X1 £	April 20X0 £
Materials	253,400	244,300
Labour	318,200	302,600
Expenses	68,700	72,400

Draw up a table showing the difference between the costs of the current month and of the corresponding month in £s, and as a percentage of the April 20X0 costs.

Question 15

Given below are the budgeted and actual costs for the two production cost centres of a business for May 20X1.

	Budget £	Actual £
Cost centre 1		
Materials	48,700	46,230
Labour	37,600	39,940
Expenses	5,200	3,700
Cost centre 2		
Materials	56,200	62,580
Labour	22,500	20,400
Expenses	4,800	5,600

You are required to draw up a table showing the amount of the variances for the month. You are also to indicate which variances should be reported to management if it is the business's policy to report only variances that are more than 15% of the budgeted figure.

Scenario Based Question 16

This scenario based question is divided into three tasks and contains various pieces of data which you may need to complete the tasks. You are advised to read the whole of the material before commencing the tasks.

Data

Classic Pine Ltd is a manufacturer and distributor of pine furniture. Classic Pine Ltd has several sites around Europe and the UK, including one in Cambridge. You work for Victor Kawabe in the accounts department of the Cambridge branch. Your duties include preparing periodic performance reports for internal consumption.

Task 1

Here are Classic Pine Ltd's quarterly sales results for the three years from 20X5.

Year	Quarter	Sales £
20X5	1	130,000
	2	120,000
	3	125,000
	4	145,000
20X6	1	140,000
	2	110,000
	3	100,000
	4	150,000
20X7	1	160,000
	2	120,000
	3	110,000
	4	170,000

Draw up a graph with sales on the vertical (y) axis and time along the horizontal (x) axis. Make sure that the scale on the y axis is such that a difference of only £2,500 is visible. (Note that this doesn't mean you have to show every multiple of £2,500 on your scale, just that the scale has to be large enough for such a difference to show.) Plot the sales figures for these three years and join the points to give a graph of quarterly sales figures against time. What comments do you have on this graph? Is there any immediately visible trend in the figures?

Task 2

Victor has asked you to produce a report comparing sales between your own branch (Cambridge), the Birmingham branch and the Manchester branch. Although Classic Pine Ltd make and sell many different products, we will be concentrating on the Regency table. Here are the actual and budgeted figures for 20X8:

Location	Sales volume (units)		Unit price (£)	
Birmingham	Budgeted:	200	Budgeted:	300
	Actual:	206	Actual:	285
Cambridge	Budgeted:	150	Budgeted:	300
	Actual:	164	Actual:	320
Manchester	Budgeted:	180	Budgeted:	300
	Actual:	162	Actual:	280

Complete the sales variance analysis below.

	Birmingham £	Cambridge £	Manchester £
Budgeted sales revenue			
Actual sales revenue			
Variance	_____	_____	_____

Comment on these figures.

Task 3

Read each of these statements carefully. In each case decide whether the statement is true or false and tick the appropriate box. Give an explanation for your decision.

		True	*False*
1	Before creating a pie chart to compare sales figures in all the European branches, Classic Pine Ltd should convert all the figures to the same currency.	☐	☐
2	A deadline for an internal report is never more important than a deadline for an external report.	☐	☐
3	A bar chart cannot be used to compare profit figures between different units in an organisation.	☐	☐
4	When asked to prepare data which will be analysed on a computer, you should provide the information on a suitable computer-readable format (eg, a floppy disk), if possible.	☐	☐

Explanations

....

....

....

....

....

....

....

....

....

....

Spreadsheets (covering Chapter 11)

Question 17

The manager of a small flower shop, Petalart, is preparing a cash flow forecast for the coming three months, and has gathered the following information:

Sales in September were £3,600, and are expected to be £3,750 in each of October and November and £4,800 in December. Most customers pay when they buy, but it is estimated that 20% of the sales are made to corporate customers, who pay in the month following that of sale.

The costs of flower and other purchases account for 50% of sales values, and are paid on a cash on delivery basis. The fixed costs of the shop, staff etc come to £1,200 per month., also paid in the month they are incurred.

The bank balance at 30 September is expected to be £450.

The cash flow forecast proforma is as follows:

	October	November	December	Total
	£	£	£	£
Sales	3,750	3,750	4,800	
Receipts – from current month's sales				
- from previous month's sales				
Total receipts				
Purchase costs				
Fixed costs				
Total payments				
Net cashflow				
Bank balance b/f				
Bank balance c/f				

Set up a spreadsheet to compute the end of month cash balances, which will also allow you to answer the query "what would happen if sales were in fact only £3,000 in October and Novembers, and £3,500 in December?"

Question 18

Houses 'R' Us is an estate agent company that has four branches in Buckfordshire. The managing director is compiling a report for the employees to inform them about the branch and company results for the past quarter. He wishes to make the report as visually interesting as possible.

The value of houses sold by each branch over the past year were as follows:

Branch	Value of houses sold
	£000
Buckford	458.2
New Milton	875.4
Wycfield	512.8
Chefford	690.1

Use a spreadsheet program to produce two different visual representations of this data.

PRACTICE SIMULATION

QUESTIONS

PRACTICE SIMULATION - QUESTIONS

The situation

Your name is Candy Date and you work as an accounts assistant in the administration department of 'Cards-R-Us', a producer of greeting cards.

You report to the management accountant, Thelma Jones. Your work is on a monthly cycle, with other projects being given to you by Thelma Jones at various times. Your main tasks are coding income and expenditure from all source documents and preparing performance reports. A junior assistant, Liam Green, sometimes helps you during busy periods.

Today's date is 12 September 20X3.

'Cards-R-Us' makes three types of cards:

- Birthday cards
- Christmas cards
- Special occasion cards

Sales are recorded in the following profit centres:

- United Kingdom
- Europe
- USA
- Rest of the World

Production is organised into the following cost centres:

- Printing
- Cutting
- Wrapping
- Packing

Production is serviced by the following cost centres:

- Administration
- Stores
- Marketing and distribution
- Maintenance

The coding system

The coding system for the company is based on a three-digit system.

The first digit denotes the type of income or expenditure:

1   Profit centre income
2   Cost centre expenditure
3   Asset expenditure
4   Liabilities
5   Capital

Profit centres

The profit centres are coded as follows:

110   United Kingdom
120   Europe
130   USA
140   Rest of the World

The third digit denotes the type of sale:

001   Birthday card
002   Christmas card
003   Special occasion cards

This means that the sale of birthday cards in Europe would be coded 121.

Cost centres

The cost centres are coded as follows:

210   Printing
220   Cutting
230   Wrapping
240   Packing
250   Administration
260   Stores
270   Marketing and distribution
280   Maintenance

The third digit donates the type of expenditure:

001   Material
002   Labour
003   Expenses

This means that the rent expenditure of the wrapping department would be 233.

Performance reports

The performance reports that you prepare on a monthly basis are for the:

◆   Management accountant
◆   Sales director
◆   Production director
◆   Cost centre managers
◆   Profit centre managers

The tasks to be completed

Task 1

Refer to the sales and purchases invoices (item 1).

Code these invoices by completing the coding extract for income and expenditure (item 5). For each relevant code you should post the amendment and update the balance. Ignore the VAT element (this is coded automatically upon receipt of the invoice).

Task 2

You receive the memo (item 2) from a cost centre manager about a wage payment that has been missed in the packing department for the month of August 20X3.

Read the memo and then do the following:

♦   Complete the wage payment schedule (item 6) to the nearest penny.
♦   Amend the coding extract (item 5) and update the relevant codes to the nearest £.

Note: Basic pay coded to labour and other employee costs are expenses.

Task 3

Liam Green has left on your desk the three invoices shown (item 4) together with the note shown (item 3).

Review the note and the three invoices and then write a memo to Liam Green. The memo should advise him:

♦   of any mistakes in checking and coding that have been made.

♦   of the appropriate persons that he needs to contact to get the information to carry out the correct coding.

Date the memo 12 September 20X3.

Task 4

In item 7 you will find a list of ledger balances for the year to date to 31 July 20X3.

Update this to 31 August 20X3 by posting the amended coding extract that you have completed in item 5.

Task 5

Using your answer from Task 4, complete the performance report for total costs of the production cost centres in item 8.

Task 6

Thelma has asked that you report to her any production cost variance of more than 10% from budget, either for the year to date or for the month of August 20X3.

Using your answer to Task 5, complete the discrepancy (variance) report (item 9), and then use the comment section to identify the significant variances that Thelma has asked for.

Task 7

Using your answer to Task 4, complete the sales performance report for total sales (item 10).

Task 8

Joan Standard, the Sales Director, is new in the post and the sales performance report that you completed in Task 7 and sent to her is the first that she has received from you. Liam has taken a message from her asking you to phone her back to tell her:

♦   what you see as the key purpose of the report.
♦   what uses it can be put to.
♦   what other information can be provided from the data that you have available.

List the key points that you see as the basis of the telephone conversation that you will have with her.

ITEM 1 – SALES AND PURCHASE INVOICES

'CARDS R US'			
SAFFRON DRIVE		VAT:	241162208
WEST WALFORD		TEL NO:	07 421 316
SALOPS		FAX NO:	07 421 317
SA4 9LK		TAX POINT:	30 AUG 20X3

SALES INVOICE

INVOICE NO: 28417

TO
CARD WAREHOUSE LTD
18 ROLLOVER DRIVE
TOSCAN
WORKBURG   USA

DETAILS	NO	NET £	TOTAL £
Type A Birthday Cards	2,000	0.80	1,600.00
Type C Wedding Cards	3,000	1.00	3,000.00
TOTAL BEFORE VAT			4,600.00
VAT			0.00
TOTAL INCLUDING VAT			4,600.00

'CARDS R US'			
SAFFRON DRIVE		VAT:	241162208
WEST WALFORD		TEL NO:	07 421 316
SALOPS		FAX NO:	07 421 317
SA4 9LK		TAX POINT:	30 AUG 20X3

SALES INVOICE

INVOICE NO: 29124

TO
SURESHOP LTD
17 RUE DU PARIS
PARIS
FRANCE

DETAILS	NO	NET £	TOTAL £
Type C Christmas Cards	2,000	0.85	1,700.00
Type D Engagement Cards	4,000	0.95	3,800.00
TOTAL BEFORE VAT			5,500.00
VAT			0.00
TOTAL INCLUDING VAT			5,500.00

TRANWAY PRINTING
35 Holding Way
Whippleton
Leics
LE9 2NR

Invoice No:	6195
VAT No:	246 368 241
Tax Point:	30/08/20X3
Tel No:	01567 78645
Fax No:	01567 78646

INVOICE TO

Cards R Us
Saffron Drive
West Walford
Salops
SA4 9LJ

	£
100 rolls of cards at £8.90 per roll, to be delivered to your Cutting Department	890.00
300 fabric prints at £2.50 per print, to be delivered to your Print Department	750.00
VAT	287.00
Total including VAT	1,927.00

D A Associates
22 Catlin Road
York Avenue
Maidstone
Kent   MA9 4CL

Invoice No:	2167
VAT No:	310 861 143
Tax Point:	26/08/20X3
Tel No:	01234 862178
Fax No:	01234 862179

INVOICE TO

Cards R Us
Saffron Drive
West Walford
Salops
SA4 9LJ

	£
Maintenance Contract for the machines in your Wrapping Department, for the year ending 31 July 20X4	1,500.00
VAT	262.50
Total including VAT	1,762.50

ITEM 2 – MEMO

MEMO

To:　　　Candy Date, Accounts Assistant

From:　　John Steel, Packing Department Manager

Date:　　11 September 20X3

Subject:　Missed wage payment

We missed a wage payment for John White, an operative on one of our packing machines, for the last week of August 20X3. He worked 35 hours at a rate of £8 per hour and then did 8 hours of overtime at time and a half to clear a general backlog.

Please calculate and code the basic wage payment and employee costs and then pass the details on to the payroll department for the personal deductions. He is a full-time employee so the employer's pension contribution of 6% of basic wage payment applies, as does the employer's national insurance contribution of 12% above £84 per week.

Thanks.

ITEM 3 – NOTE

NOTEPAD

Candy

I have just checked and coded the attached invoices for September 20X3 but I am not sure whether the action I have taken is correct. Please help!

Liam

ITEM 4 – INVOICES

Ince and Sons Brokers

	Invoice No:　　2167
2 Lambert Avenue Bristol BR9 6EL	Tel No:　　　01717 733451

Invoice to: Cards R Us Saffron Drive West Walford Salops SA4 9LK	213

Provision of insurance for your factory for the year ending 30 September 20X4	£6,000.00

Aftercare Limited

13 Carson Road
London
SN4 0EL

Invoice No: 1468
VAT No: 789 453 292
Tax Point: 11 Sept 20X3
Tel No: 020 7941 367

Invoice to:
Cards Delight
27 Wapping Lane
Portsmouth
Hants
PO1 9FM

(253)

Provision of temporary staff for your Admin Department
8 days at £150 per day   £1,200.00

Cellplate Ltd

Unit 6
Dockway Drive
Liverpool   LA4 5XF

Invoice No: 4736
VAT No: 241 074 375
Tax Point: 4 Sept 20X3
Tel No: 0151 441 857

Invoice to:
Cards R Us
Saffron Drive
West Walford
Salops
SA4 9LK

(231)

48 boxes of wrapping material at £25 per box   £12,000

ITEM 5 (FOR TASK 1)

CODING EXTRACT – INCOME AND EXPENDITURE – AUGUST 20X3

(ROUNDED TO NEAREST £)

Code	Balance (£)	Amendment (£)	Updated balance (£)
111	38,916		
112	27,413		
113	33,476		
121	42,457		
122	29,376		
123	24,294		
131	38,462		
132	34,761		
133	37,314		
141	41,694		
142	52,316		
143	45,761		
211	47,412		
212	11,467		
213	20,439		
221	43,764		
222	11,461		
223	15,064		
231	8,216		
232	4,916		
233	9,074		
241	3,642		
242	4,164		
243	7,695		
253	6,613		
263	7,008		
273	6,744		
283	4,539		

ITEM 6 (FOR TASK 2)

<table>
<tr><td colspan="4" align="center">PAYROLL CALCULATION
AUGUST 20X3</td></tr>
<tr><td>NAME</td><td colspan="3"></td></tr>
<tr><td>DEPARTMENT</td><td colspan="3"></td></tr>
<tr><td>BASIC RATE</td><td colspan="3"></td></tr>
<tr><td>HOURS WORKED</td><td colspan="3"></td></tr>
<tr><td>HOURS FOR OVERTIME PREMIUM</td><td colspan="3"></td></tr>
<tr><td></td><td>Calculation</td><td>Amount (£)</td><td>Code</td></tr>
<tr><td>BASIC RATE</td><td></td><td></td><td></td></tr>
<tr><td>OVERTIME PREMIUM</td><td></td><td></td><td></td></tr>
<tr><td>EMPLOYERS PENSION CONT</td><td></td><td></td><td></td></tr>
<tr><td>EMPLOYERS NIC</td><td></td><td></td><td></td></tr>
<tr><td>TOTALS FOR POSTING</td><td colspan="2" align="center">Code</td><td>Amount (£)</td></tr>
<tr><td></td><td colspan="2"></td><td></td></tr>
</table>

ITEM 7 (FOR TASK 4)

INCOME AND EXPENDITURE BALANCES – Year ending 31/12/20X3

Ledger account	Balance at 31/7/20X3 £	Amount coded August 20X3 £	Balance at 31/8/20X3 £
Sales			
Birthday cards			
- UK	245,365		
- Europe	198,467		
- USA	231,989		
- Rest of World	297,946		
Christmas cards			
- UK	246,578		
- Europe	316,478		
- USA	297,697		
- Rest of World	399,906		
Special Cards			
- UK	198,464		
- Europe	201,897		
- USA	246,890		
- Rest of World	299,785		
Expenditure			
Printing			
- Material	74,789		
- Labour	61,890		
- Expenses	93,167		
Cutting			
- Material	71,789		
- Labour	58,625		
- Expenses	75,293		
Wrapping			
- Material	58,693		
- Labour	31,704		
- Expenses	34,471		
Packing			
- Material	38,568		
- Labour	36,906		
- Expenses	48,966		

ITEM 8 (FOR TASK 5)

PERFORMANCE REPORT PRODUCTION COST CENTRES TOTAL COSTS – AUGUST 20X3				
	MONTH – AUG 20X3		YEAR TO DATE	
	Actual £	Budget £	Actual £	Budget £
Material		108,500		341,700
Labour		32,250		198,500
Expenses		48,750		277,100

ITEM 9 (FOR TASK 6)

DISCREPANCY (VARIANCE) REPORT PRODUCTION COST CENTRES AUGUST 20X3		
PERIOD COST	MONTH £	YEAR TO DATE £
Material		
Labour		
Expenses		
COMMENT		

ITEM 10 (FOR TASK 7)

SALES PERFORMANCE REPORT – AUGUST 20X3				
PERIOD PROFIT CENTRE	MONTH ACTUAL	MONTH BUDGET	YEAR TO DATE ACTUAL	YEAR TO DATE BUDGET
	£	£	£	£
UNITED KINGDOM		98,000		785,000
EUROPE		109,000		832,500
USA		112,800		886,400
REST OF WORLD		142,100		1,164,000

MOCK SIMULATION 1

QUESTIONS

MOCK SIMULATION 1

DATA AND TASKS

Introduction

The situation is set out below, followed by the tasks which you are required to complete.

You should read the whole simulation before commencing work so as to gain an overall picture of what is required.

Your answer should be set out in the answer booklet provided.

You are allowed **three hours** to complete your work.

A high level of accuracy is required. Check your work carefully.

The situation

Your name is Jarem Zareere and you work for Shezad Malik, the owner director of Crescent Taxis Ltd. Shezad formed his business some 10 years ago in the North East of England. He now has branches of the business in Scarborough, Filey, Bridlington and Whitby. He employs a staff of 40 and has a fleet of 36 vehicles.

The company has a small workshop in Whitby where the taxis are serviced and maintained. There is also a central stores at the premises.

You are employed as an accounting technician reporting directly to Shezad. Your work focuses on the monthly management accounting cycle. Some of your duties include coding income and expenditure from a range of source documents and preparing period performance reports. The accounts section is based in Whitby.

The company branches are classed as responsibility centres and comprise:

♦ Bridlington
♦ Filey
♦ Scarborough
♦ Whitby

The time is late June 20X2 and the company has a 31 December year end.

The company has three main categories of business:

♦ Short runs – local.

♦ Longer runs – clients to airports.

♦ Contracts – there is a contract with a local authority education department to transport disabled students from their home to school/college, and also contracts with local nursing homes and hotels.

Each branch is divided into cost centres and is supported by service cost centres:

♦ Reception/office
♦ Taxi fleet vehicles
♦ Maintenance workshop – Whitby
♦ Stores – Whitby
♦ Accounts department – Whitby

The coding system

The system is based on a six digit structure.

Both revenue from turnover and expenditure are analysed to responsibility centre and business type; the first three digits identify the responsibility centre and the second three, the category of business.

Responsibility centre

100	Bridlington
110	Filey
120	Scarborough
130	Whitby

Category of business

001	Short run – local
002	Longer run – airports
003	Contract work

Thus contract work for a local nursing home at the Whitby branch would be coded as:

130.003

Cost centres

These are coded as:

150	Reception/office
160	Taxi fleet vehicles
170	Maintenance workshop
180	Stores
190	Accounts/admin

The first and second digit denote the cost centre and the third digit the expenditure classification:

001	Direct labour
002	Direct materials and direct costs – fuel, tyres
003	Indirect labour
004	Indirect materials including oils and greases
005	Overheads including maintenance
006	Capital expenditure

Thus the cost of drivers' wages at the Whitby branch would be coded as:

130.161

VAT

VAT is coded as:

197

130. - - - (coded to Whitby accounts department)

007   Input tax

There is no output tax on the turnover – assume this is an exempt supply.

Tasks for completion

Task 1

Refer to the sales invoices and takings summary following these tasks, together with the purchase invoices, and prepare the coding of these source documents by completing the coding extracts in the answer booklet in the space provided.

Task 2

Once you have coded the sales invoices and takings summary, you are required to complete the income analysis for the period and then compare the budget with the actual turnover showing the variance (difference) for each code and in total.

The proforma for this summary is provided in the answer booklet.

Task 3

Having completed the comparison in Task 2 above, you are required to calculate the percentage increase or decrease in turnover compared to budget for each code and in total, and summarise your results on the report form provided in the answer booklet.

Task 4

Shezad usually completes the weekly wages for each branch and has processed the gross wages for all the branches except Whitby for the week ended 30 June 20X2.

He has been called away and leaves you a note regarding the wages for Whitby employees.

The note from Shezad is shown in the data below, following the sales invoices and other source documents.

Read the note, calculate the gross wages and complete the coding extract provided in the answer booklet, together with the summary of gross pay.

Task 5

The summary of actual gross wages to date is provided in the answer booklet. Complete the report to 30 June 20X2.

Task 6

The comparative summary of budget to actual gross pay for each branch is provided in the answer booklet.

Complete the summary showing clearly budget, actual and variance for the period, together with the percentage increase or decrease over budget.

Task 7

Shezad has recently introduced a central stores system for some materials required by the branches.

In the data below you will find a number of material requisitions for the week ended 30 June 20X2.

Code these issues and complete the coding schedule provided in the answer booklet, showing both £ and pence.

Task 8

The petty cash for each branch is administered in the branch reception/office. One of your duties is to periodically check the petty cash control at each branch.

You call in at the Bridlington branch and check the petty cash records. Because of pressure of work and sick leave this current week, the receptionist has not coded the expenditure and the return is due in to you at Whitby. In order to complete this on time, you decide to code the expenditure on the vouchers for the current week.

Refer to the petty cash vouchers in the data below, code the expenditure, and prepare the analysis summary provided in the answer booklet, showing both £ and pence.

Task 9

On recent visits to branches you have noticed that on some occasions both petty cash vouchers and material requisition notes have not been signed.

Write one memo to all branch receptionists regarding the petty cash vouchers and a further memo to Bill Gull, the employee responsible for stock control, with reference to the material requisitions, expressing the need for signatures on these documents.

Use the space provided in the answer booklet. Your memos should be dated 30 June 20X2.

Data

**SALES INVOICES, TAKINGS SUMMARY AND
PURCHASE INVOICES – WEEK ENDED 30 JUNE 20X2** *contract*

Crescent Taxis Ltd	VAT No: 9371276
The Crescent	Tel No: 01947 871232
Whitby	Fax No: 01947 871233
YO21 3JZ	Tax point: 30 June 20X2

Sales Invoice

Hawsker Nursing Home
Raw Lane
Whitby
YO21 7P2

No: 02/921
Your order: HNH 73

To: Taxi service for residents for period ended 30 June 20X2.

Service supplied from Whitby branch. £275.00

Per attached listing *code: 130.003*

100.003

Crescent Taxis Ltd	VAT No: 9371276
The Crescent	Tel No: 01947 871232
Whitby	Fax No: 01947 871233
YO21 3JZ	Tax point: 30 June 20X2

Sales Invoice

Bridlington Hall School
Filey Lane
Bridlington   No: 02/922
YO30 0KL   Your order: 1724

To: Taxi service for disabled students as per contract – June 20X2.

        Service supplied from Bridlington branch.   £480.00

110.003

Crescent Taxis Ltd	VAT No: 9371276
The Crescent	Tel No: 01947 871232
Whitby	Fax No: 01947 871233
YO21 3JZ	Tax point: 30 June 20X2

Sales Invoice

Filey Vale Private Hospital
Thirsk Road
Filey   No: 02/924
YO36 3ZP   Your order: FPH 79

To: Taxi service for private patients per contract – June 20X2.

        Service supplied by Filey branch.   £175.00

120.003

Crescent Taxis Ltd	VAT No: 9371276
The Crescent	Tel No: 01947 871232
Whitby	Fax No: 01947 871233
YO21 3JZ	Tax point: 30 June 20X2

Sales Invoice

Bay City Hotel
High Street
Scarborough   No: 02/925
YO24 0LX   Your order: 792

To: Taxi service for hotel guests per contract – June 20X2.

        Service supplied by Scarborough branch.   £127.00

CASH TAKINGS SUMMARY
WEEK ENDED 30 JUNE 20X2

			£
Bridlington :	100.001	Short run – local	5,040 ✓
	100.002	Longer runs	450
Filey :	110.001	Short run – local	5,300
	110.002	Longer runs	410
Scarborough :	120.001	Short run – local	5,437
	120.002	Longer runs	690
Whitby :	130.001	Short run – local	5,525
	130.002	Longer runs	710
			£23,562

PURCHASE INVOICES

NE Fuel & Garages
Grape Lane
Scarborough
YO24 3JZ

VAT No:	927 6132
Tel No:	01923 817911
Fax No:	01923 817912
Tax point:	30 June 20X2

Invoice

Crescent Taxis Ltd
The Crescent
Whitby
YO21 3JZ

Invoice No:	NE 1792
Your order:	791

	£	
To: Supply of petrol for June 20X2 per attached list.		
Bridlington Branch	3,250.00	100.162
Filey Branch	3,410.00	110.162
Scarborough Branch	3,517.00	120.162
Whitby Branch	3,323.00	130.162
	13,500.00	
VAT 17½%	2,362.50	130.197
	£15,862.50	

Loftus Insurance Services
Cayton Lane
Whitby
YO21 3HZ

VAT No:	9221937
Tel No:	01947 711613
Fax No:	01947 711614
Tax point:	30 June 20X2

Invoice

Crescent Taxis Ltd
The Crescent
Whitby
YO21 3JZ

Invoice No:	9172
Your order:	653

£ - p

To: Renewal of block policy for insurance on taxi fleet vehicles.

100.165 Bridlington Branch   5,850.00
110. 165 Filey Branch   6,150.00
120. 165 Scarborough Branch   6,350.00
130. 165 Whitby Branch   5,950.00
                                                    _____
                                                    £24,300.00
                                                    _____

        Per attached schedule.

Raw Garage Supplies
Filey Lane
Scarborough
YO24 1LP

VAT No:	8727961
Tel No:	01923 827913
Fax No:	01923 827914
Tax point:	30 June 20X2

Invoice

Crescent Taxis Ltd
The Crescent
Whitby
YO21 3JZ

Invoice No:	9176
Your order:	657

Description	Unit quantity	Unit price	Total £
Engine oil general purpose	5 x 10 litre packs	£20 per pack	100.00
VAT AT 17½%			17.50
			_____
			£117.50
			_____

130.174

130.197

direct materials

Delivered to Whitby workshop.

Filey Office Supplies
The Marine Way
Filey
YO27 1PT

VAT No:	8976123
Tel No:	01923 721672
Fax No:	01923 729112
Tax point:	30 June 20X2

Invoice

Crescent Taxis Ltd
The Crescent
Whitby
YO21 3JZ

Invoice No:	F0S 9714
Your order:	661

116.156

To: Supply one XJ3 photocopier and accessories.

130.197

Special contract price	£450.00
VAT 17.5%	£78.75
	£528.75

CAPITAL

Delivered to Filey branch reception.

PED Motor Supplies
Upgery Lane
Whitby
YO21 3ZP

VAT No:	9217893
Tel No:	01947 825430
Fax No:	01947 825431
Tax point:	30 June 20X2

Invoice

Crescent Taxis Ltd
The Crescent
Whitby
YO21 3JZ

Invoice No:	PED 796
Your order:	663

Description	Unit quantity	Unit price	Total £
Car valet cleaning packs	100	£0.75 each	75.00
Cleaning cloths	100	£0.20 each	20.00
			£95.00
VAT 17½%			16.62
			£111.62

30.184
30.684
130.197

Indirect materials.

Delivered to Central Stores, Whitby.

```
NE Coast Trader                    VAT No:       7234562
Bridlington Lane                   Tel No:       01727 969721
Filey                              Fax No:       01727 969722
YO27 3EQ                           Tax point:    30 June 20X2
```

Invoice

```
Crescent Taxis Ltd
The Crescent
Whitby                             Invoice No:   8134
YO21 3JZ                           Your order:   659
```

To:	Advert in trade – 4 issues – June 20X2.	
	Per special price	£140.00
	VAT 17½%	24.50
		£164.50

Handwritten margin notes: 116 | 56 · 130 | 197

Filey branch advert.

NOTE FROM SHEZAD

Jarem

Please calculate the gross wages for the Whitby branch employees for the week ended 30 June 20X2.

As you are aware, the basic hourly working week is 38 hours and any hours in excess are paid as overtime at time and a half.

We operate a group bonus which is calculated as 5% of the branch's short run business. Each employee shares equally in this bonus. The bonus is paid to the nearest '£'.

The gross wages for the Whitby branch to 23 June were		£66,250	
	130.161	£54,650	*5% 2,7325*
	130.163	£11,600	

The hours worked this week per employee are:

Jane Smith	40	(reception)	*200 + 2 50 = 250 +*
Bill Brown	48		
John Dunn	48		
Pauline Jones	50		
Kathy Jones	42	(drivers)	
Jack Martin	46		
Brian Smithers	50		
William Bows	50		
John Stockdale	46		
Bill Gull	40	(workshop)	

The hourly rate is £5. You already have details of the business turnover for the week.

MATERIAL REQUISITIONS

130.184

Material requisition		No:	733
		Date:	28/6/X2

Details	Unit quantity	Price	Total
4 packs of cleaning valet materials (Whitby branch)	4	75p each	£3.00

Requested by: P Jones

Authorised by: B Gull

110.186

Material requisition		No:	734
		Date:	29/6/X2

Details	Unit quantity	Price	Total
5 packs photocopying paper (Filey branch)	5	£4.50 each	£22.50

Requested by: L Gibson

Authorised by: B Gull

100.182

Material requisition		No:	735
		Date:	30/6/X2

Details	Unit quantity	Price	Total
1 set replacement car carpets (Bridlington branch)	1	15.00	£15.00

Requested by: J Jones

Authorised by: B Gull

120. 186

Material requisition		No:	736
		Date:	30/6/X2

Details	Unit quantity	Price	Total
1 pack (5) fax rolls (Scarborough branch)	1	11.50	£11.50

Requested by: M Dean

Authorised by: B Gull

PETTY CASH VOUCHERS

Petty Cash Voucher

No: B71
Date: 26/6/X2

Description	Quantity	Price	£
Copy shop printed leaflets	1,000	£20 per 1,000	20.00
VAT			3.50
			23.50

Requested by: J Brown
Authorised by: P Dunn

Petty Cash Voucher

No: B72
Date: 27/6/X2

Description	Quantity	Price	£
Tea and coffee for reception	-	-	9.50

Requested by: J Collinson
Authorised by: P Dunn

Petty Cash Voucher			
		No:	B73
		Date:	28/6/X2
Description	*Quantity*	*Price*	*£*
Window cleaner – reception area	-	-	7.50
Requested by: *J Collinson*			
Authorised by: *P Dunn*			

Petty Cash Voucher			
		No:	B74
		Date:	29/6/X2
Description	*Quantity*	*Price*	*£*
Office/reception cleaner wages	-	-	21.50
Requested by: *B Smart*			
Authorised by: *P Dunn*			

MOCK
SIMULATION 1

ANSWER
BOOKLET

TASK 1

**ANALYSIS OF TURNOVER
WEEK ENDED 30 JUNE 20X2**

Code	£
100.001	
100.002	
100.003	
110.001	
110.002	
110.003	
120.001	
120.002	
120.003	
130.001	
130.002	
130.003	
	£

**CODING EXTRACT - PURCHASES
WEEK ENDED 30 JUNE 20X2**

(to nearest '£')

	£
100.162	
100.165	
110.155	
110.156	
110.162	
110.165	
120.162	
120.165	
130.162	
130.165	
130.174	
130.184	
130.197	
	£

BATCH CONTROL SHEET - PURCHASE INVOICES
(show £ and pence)

£

NE Fuel & Garages

Loftus Insurance Services

Raw Garage Supplies

Filey Office Supplies

PED Motor Supplies

NE Coast Trader

£

TASK 2

ANALYSIS OF TURNOVER, BUDGET – ACTUAL
PERIOD ENDED 30 JUNE 20X2

Code	Budget to 30 June £	Actual to 23 June £	Actual w/e 30 June £	Actual to 30 June £	Variance increase/ (decrease) £
100.001	120,000	122,500			
100.002	11,000	12,300			
100.003	12,000	12,100			
110.001	132,000	129,400			
110.002	10,500	9,500			
110.003	5,000	4,100			
120.001	135,000	131,200			
120.002	15,100	14,900			
120.003	3,100	2,750			
130.001	130,000	126,000			
130.002	16,100	14,800			
130.003	5,125	4,100			
	£594,925	£583,650			

% Total increase/(decrease)   ....%

TASK 3

TURNOVER, BUDGET – ACTUAL
% COMPARISON, PERIOD ENDED 30 JUNE 20X2

Code	Budget £	Actual £	% increase/ (decrease) (to 2 decimal places)
100.001			
100.002			
100.003			
110.001			
110.002			
110.003			
120.001			
120.002			
120.003			
130.001			
130.002			
130.003			
	£594,925	£608,269	2.24%

TASK 4

WHITBY BRANCH
GROSS PAY WEEK ENDED 30 JUNE 20X2

Name	Basic hours £	Overtime £	Bonus £	Total £
J Smith				
B Brown				
J Dunn				
P Jones				
K Jones				
J Martin				
B Smithers				
W Bows				
J Stockdale				
B Gull				

Coding analysis (to nearest £)

130.161

130.163

Bonus calculation :   Turnover × 5% =   £

Bonus per employee : $\dfrac{£}{10 \text{ employees}}$ =   £

TASK 5

SUMMARY OF GROSS WAGES TO DATE
- 30 JUNE 20X2

Code	£
100.161	57,100
100.163	6,100
110.161	58,250
110.163	5,875
120.161	59,100
120.163	5,975
130.161	
130.163	
	_____
	£
	_____

TASK 6

ANALYSIS OF GROSS WAGES, BUDGET – ACTUAL
PERIOD ENDED 30 JUNE 20X2

Code	Budget	Actual	Variance increase/ (decrease)	% increase/ (decrease)
	£	£	£	%
100.161	55,000			
100.163	6,000			
110.161	58,000			
110.163	5,900			
120.161	59,500			
120.163	5,750			
130.161	57,500			
130.163	12,000			
	_____	_____	_____	_____
	£259,650	£	£	%
	_____	_____	_____	_____

TASK 7

MATERIAL REQUISITION CODING
WEEK ENDED 30 JUNE 20X2

Coding   £

                                                                    _____

                                                                    £
                                                                    _____

TASK 8

PETTY CASH VOUCHER ANALYSIS
WEEK ENDED 30 JUNE 20X2

Bridlington branch

Coding   £

                                                                    _____

                                                                    £
                                                                    _____

TASK 9

CRESCENT TAXIS LTD

MEMO

To:

From:

Date:

Subject:

CRESCENT TAXIS LTD

MEMO

To:

From:

Date:

Subject:

MOCK SIMULATION 2

QUESTIONS

MOCK SIMULATION 2

Introduction

This simulation is designed to test your ability to supply information for management control.

The situation is set out below, followed by the tasks which you are required to complete.

You should read the whole simulation before commencing work so as to gain an overall picture of what is required.

Your answer should be set out in the answer booklet provided.

You are allowed **three hours** to complete your work.

A high level of accuracy is required. Check your work carefully.

The situation

Your name is Sammy Jetson and you work as an accounts assistant in the administration department of Fantastic Frames, a manufacturer of photograph frames.

You report to the management accountant, Fred Wilcox. Your main tasks are the coding of income and expenses from source documents and preparing a variety of month end performance reports.

Fantastic Frames sells three types of photograph frame:

♦ silver plate

♦ wood

♦ gilt

Sales are expanding into Europe and are recorded in the following profit centres:

♦ United Kingdom

♦ France

♦ Spain

♦ Rest of Europe

Production takes place in the following cost centres:

♦ cutting

♦ assembly

♦ painting

♦ packing

Production is serviced by the following cost centres:

♦ stores

♦ maintenance

♦ sales and marketing

♦ administration

The coding system

All income and expenditure is coded according to the profit centre or cost centre to which it relates, and the type of income or expenditure. All income and expenditure is coded using a five digit code.

The first digit denotes the type of income or expenditure as follows:

1   cost centre expenditure

2   profit centre income

3   asset expenditure

4   liabilities

5   capital and drawings

The next two digits denote the profit centre or cost centre to which the income or expenditure relates as follows:

Profit centres:

01   United Kingdom

02   France

03   Spain

04   Rest of Europe

Cost centres:

01   Cutting

02   Assembly

03   Painting

04   Packing

05   Stores

06   Maintenance

07   Sales and marketing

08   Administration

The final two digits denote the type of income or expense:

Sales income:

11   Silver plate frames

12   Wood frames

13   Gilt frames

Expenditure:

21   Materials

22   Labour

23   Expenses

Examples of the coding at work are:

♦   sales of wood frames in France would be coded as 20212;

♦   the purchase of materials for use in the cutting department would be coded as 10121.

THE TASKS TO BE COMPLETED

TASK 1

Refer to the sales and purchases invoices on the following pages.

Code each of the invoices in the blank code box on the face of the invoice. You can ignore any VAT element as this is coded automatically.

TASK 2

Refer to the coding extract for income and expenditure for the month of June 20X1 in the answer booklet. For each of the invoices coded in Task 1 you are required to enter the additional amounts in the amendment column and update the balance.

TASK 3

You have received a memo from Fred Wilcox regarding the June wage payment for a new employee in the assembly department whose wage payment was not processed with the rest of the June wages.

Read the memo and then:

♦ complete the payroll calculation schedule given in the answer booklet to the nearest penny;

♦ update the relevant codes on the coding extract used for Task 2 showing the amended balance to the nearest £.

Note: Basic pay is dealt with as a labour cost whilst all other employee costs are dealt with as expenses.

TASK 4

In the answer booklet you will find the coding extract for the year to date as at 30 June 20X1.

Update this coding extract for all of the income and expense codes with the June figures taken from the updated coding extract for June used earlier.

TASK 5

Using your answer to Task 4 complete the performance report for total costs of the production cost centres given in the answer booklet.

TASK 6

You are required to report any production cost variances which are more than 10% of budget, either for the month or for the year to date, to Fred Wilcox.

Using the answer to Task 5 complete the variance report given in the answer booklet and then use the comment section to identify the variances which must be reported.

TASK 7

Using your answer to Task 4 complete the sales performance report for each of the profit centres given in the answer booklet.

TASK 8

You are required to report any sales variances which are more than 10% of budget, either for the month or for the year to date, to Fred Wilcox.

Using your answer to Task 7 complete the variance report for sales given in the answer booklet and then use the comment section to identify the variances which must be reported.

TASK 9

Using your answer to Task 4 you are now to complete the sales analysis report given in the answer booklet.

TASK 10

You are required to report any sales analysis variances which are more than 10% of budget, either for the month or for the year to date, to Fred Wilcox.

Using your answer to Task 9 complete the variance report for sales given in the answer booklet and then use the comment section to identify the variances which must be reported.

TASK 11

The Sales Director, Karen Miller, has recently joined the organisation and has asked you to a short meeting in her office in order to discuss the two sales reports from Tasks 7 and 9. Her main concerns are:

♦   what are the key purposes of each report?

♦   what are the main uses of each report?

♦   is one report more useful than the other?

You are to use the notepad given in the answer booklet to list the main points which you will cover in this meeting.

TASK 1

INVOICE

Invoice to:
E L Salons
20 Rueja Alta
Madrid
SPAIN

Fantastic Frames

Bridge Park Estate
Wallingham
NT16 4LP
Tel: 0488 611 202
Fax: 0488 611 203

Invoice no: 26719
Tax point: 30 June 20X1
VAT reg no: 384 6113 97

Code	*Description*	*Quantity*	*VAT rate* %	*Unit price* £	*Amount exclusive of VAT* £
G12P	Gilt Frame	250	17.5	16.40	4,100.00
S07A	Silver plate frame	180	17.5	9.20	1,656.00
					5,756.00
VAT at 17.5%		Code:			1,007.30
Total amount payable					6,763.30

INVOICE

<table>
<tr><td>

Invoice to:
Humbug Stores
Victoria Place
Wilton
Cheshire
England

</td><td>

Fantastic Frames

Bridge Park Estate
Wallingham
NT16 4LP
Tel: 0488 611 202
Fax: 0488 611 203

Invoice no: 26720
Tax point: 30 June 20X1
VAT reg no: 384 6113 97

</td></tr>
</table>

Code	Description	Quantity	VAT rate %	Unit price £	Amount exclusive of VAT £
W61T	Wood frame	40	17.5	18.80	752.00
S11L	Silver plate frame	25	17.5	12.60	315.00

	1,067.00
VAT at 17.5% Code:	186.72
Total amount payable	1,253.72

INVOICE

Invoice to:
Fantastic Frames
Bridge Park Estate
Wallingham
NT16 4LP

T J Wood Supplies

Porter House
Wallingham
NT4 6NT

Invoice no:	F4712
Tax point:	27 June 20X1
VAT reg no:	462 3779 14

Code	Description	Quantity	VAT rate %	Unit price £	Amount exclusive of VAT £
PT410	Stripped Pine	140 m	17.5	6.25	875.00
M2623	Mahogany	85 m	17.5	9.20	782.00
					1,657.00

VAT at 17.5%

Total amount payable

Code:

289.97

1,946.97

INVOICE

Specialist Paints

28/32 Upper Street
Fairborough
NT23 0LP

Invoice to:
Fantastic Frames
Bridge Park Estate
Wallingham
NT16 4LP

Invoice no:	6124
Tax point:	26 June 20X1
VAT reg no:	442 3791 88

Code	Description	Quantity	VAT rate %	Unit price £	Amount exclusive of VAT £
2461	Gold Paint	20 litres	17.5	15.80	316.00
					316.00

VAT at 17.5%

Code:

55.30

Total amount payable

371.30

TASK 3

MEMO

TO:	Sammy Jetson
FROM:	Fred Wilcox
DATE:	30 June 20X1
SUBJECT:	Wage payment

A new employee in the assembly department, Lillian Frant, has not had her wages processed with the rest of the payroll. She only joined the business at the start of the last week in June and in that week worked for 42 hours. She has joined the company pension scheme.

The basic week is 35 hours and Lillian's basic rate of pay is £9.40 per hour with time and a half paid for overtime hours. The employer's contribution to the pension scheme is 5% of basic pay and the employer's national insurance contributions are 12.5% of weekly pay above £84.

MOCK
SIMULATION 2

ANSWER
BOOKLET

TASKS 2 AND 3

Coding extract – income and expenditure – June 20X1 (Rounded to the nearest £)

Code	Balance £	Amendment £	Updated balance £
10121	76,395		
10122	24,576		
10123	8,146		
10221	13,574		
10222	64,685		
10223	9,326		
10321	23,465		
10322	57,689		
10323	6,275		
10421	18,765		
10422	15,781		
10423	10,367		
10522	18,254		
10523	3,255		
10622	19,370		
10623	4,174		
10722	70,325		
10723	26,485		
10822	61,350		
10823	57,385		
20111	95,327		
20112	86,790		
20113	88,264		
20211	67,375		
20212	71,484		
20213	62,549		
20311	54,185		
20312	39,265		
20313	42,465		
20411	18,478		
20412	20,365		
20413	17,363		

TASK 3

Payroll calculation schedule – June 20X1

NAME

DEPARTMENT

BASIC RATE

TOTAL HOURS WORKED

OVERTIME HOURS WORKED

	Calculation	Amount £	Code
BASIC PAY			
OVERTIME PREMIUM			
EMPLOYER'S PENSION CONT			
EMPLOYER'S NIC			
		————	
TOTALS FOR POSTING (£)			
		————	

TASK 4

Code	Balance at 31 May £	June figures £	Updated balance at 30 June £
10121	228,310		
10122	71,254		
10123	24,165		
10221	38,450		
10222	193,272		
10223	27,364		
10321	69,264		
10322	171,264		
10323	18,325		
10421	55,163		
10422	42,673		
10423	28,663		
10522	56,264		
10523	9,265		
10622	57,265		
10623	12,574		
10722	209,436		
10723	78,412		
10822	183,562		
10823	172,563		
20111	296,385		
20112	258,233		
20113	264,264		
20211	201,573		
20212	215,265		
20213	186,254		
20311	158,325		
20312	117,637		
20313	127,254		
20411	53,672		
20412	60,261		
20413	47,365		

Title row: **Coding extract – income and expenditure – year to 30 June 20X1 (Rounded to the nearest £)**

TASK 5

Performance report – production cost centres – total costs				
June 20X1				
	Month – June 20X1		Year to date	
	Actual	Budget	Actual	Budget
	£	£	£	£
Materials		120,350		476,900
Labour		170,560		722,400
Expenses		31,600		130,500

TASK 6

Variance report – production cost centres – June 20X1		
	Month	Year to date
	£	£
Materials		
Labour		
Expenses		
Comment		

TASK 7

Sales performance report – June 20X1				
	Month – June 20X1		**Year to date**	
	Actual £	**Budget** £	**Actual** £	**Budget** £
United Kingdom		290,500		1,250,000
France		190,300		740,200
Spain		120,000		440,000
Rest of Europe		61,200		200,000

TASK 8

Variance report – sales – June 20X1		
	Month £	**Year to date** £
United Kingdom		
France		
Spain		
Rest of Europe		

Comment

TASK 9

Sales analysis report – June 20X1

	Month – June 20X1		Year to date	
	Actual £	Budget £	Actual £	Budget £
Silver plate frames		213,000		895,000
Wood frames		235,000		950,000
Gilt frames		194,000		755,000

TASK 10

Variance report – sales analysis – June 20X1

	Month £	Year to date £
Silver plate frames		
Wood frames		
Gilt frames		

Comment

TASK 11

NOTEPAD

ANSWERS

KEY TECHNIQUES – ANSWERS

Principles of cost accounting (covering Chapters 1 and 2)

Answer 1

(i)   Fixed

(ii)   Variable

(iii)   Variable

(iv)   Fixed

Answer 2

(i)   010631

(ii)   030521

(iii)   010412

(iv)   030632

(v)   020522

(vi)   020633

Materials and labour costs (covering Chapters 3 and 4)

Answer 3

Stores record card										
MATERIAL DESCRIPTION										
Code			ZZ410							
Date	*Receipts*			*Issues*			*Balance*			
	Quantity			*Quantity*			*Quantity*			
01/05							30			
03/05	200						230			
05/05				160			70			
10/05	180						250			
11/05				180			70			
12/05				40			30			
20/05	240						270			
21/05				200			70			
23/05	30						100			
26/05	200						300			
30/05				220			80			

Answer 4

(i)   £225 + £120 + £26   =   £371

(ii)   £225 + £96   =   £321

(iii)   £225 + £48   =   £273, adjusted to £285 guaranteed minimum

Answer 5

	Gross pay	Overtime premium
(i)	(40 hrs × £6.20) + £6.20 overtime premium = £254.20	2 hrs × £6.20 × ½ = £6.20
(ii)	(46 hrs × £6.20) + £24.80 overtime premium = £310.00	8 hrs × £6.20 × ½ = £24.80
(iii)	(43 hrs × £6.20) + £15.50 overtime premium = £282.10	5 hrs × £6.20 × ½ = £15.50

Expenses and sales (covering Chapters 5 and 6)

Answer 6

Plant and machinery   20% × £15,200   =   £3,040

Motor vehicles   20% × £16,500   =   £3,300

Answer 7

Task 1

	RECEIPTS				ISSUES				STOCK		
Date	GRN No	Quantity	Unit price £	Amount £	Stores Req No	Quantity	Unit price £	Amount £	Quantity	Unit price £	Amount £
Dec 1									24		
Dec 2	101	96							96		
									120		
									—		
Dec 4					2	24					
						24					
						—					
						48			72		
						—					
Dec 6	103	72							72		
									144		
Dec 7	106	24							24		
									168		
									—		
Dec 8					6	72					
						24			48		
						—			24		
						96			—		
						—			72		
									—		
Dec 9					10	24			24		
									24		
									—		
									48		
									—		
Dec 10					12	24			24		

STORES RECORD CARD
Material: Frame .... Code: 3264
Supplier: T Mayer Ltd ....

STORES RECORD CARD

Material: Frame.. Code: 1638

Supplier: ABT Ltd......................................

Date	RECEIPTS				ISSUES				STOCK		
	GRN No	Quantity	Unit price £	Amount £	Stores Req No	Quantity	Unit price £	Amount £	Quantity	Unit price £	Amount £
Dec 1									72		
Dec 4	102	96							96		
									168		
Dec 6	104	96							96		
									264		
Dec 7					5	72			48		
						48			96		
						120			144		
Dec 8	107	96							96		
									240		
Dec 9					8	48			24		
						72			96		
						120			120		
Dec 9					11	24			96		

STORES RECORD CARD

Material: Divider.. Code: 364

Supplier: Shine Ltd ....

	RECEIPTS				ISSUES				STOCK		
Date	GRN No	Quantity	Unit price £	Amount £	Stores Req No	Quantity	Unit price £	Amount £	Quantity	Unit price £	Amount £
Dec 1									480 ⎯		
Dec 4					1	240			240 ⎯		
Dec 6					3	96			144 ⎯		
Dec 7					4	12			132		
Dec 7	105	600							600		
									732 ⎯		
Dec 8					7	132 60 ⎯ 192 ⎯			540 ⎯		
Dec 9					9	288			252		
Dec 10	108	600							600		
									852 ⎯		

Answer 8

	£	£
Sales		568,000
Less: costs		
Cost of goods	390,000	
Sales force's wages	88,000	
Sales force's expenses	6,000	
Sales force's commission	24,000	
Advertising	18,000	
		(526,000)
Profit		42,000

Methods of reporting and presenting information (covering Chapters 7 and 8)

Answer 9

(i)   Note or e-mail

(ii)   Report

(iii)   Memo or e-mail

(iv)   Letter

Answer 10

TABLE OF QUARTERLY SALES

	Current quarter (1/X1 – 3/X1) £	Previous quarter (10/X0 – 12/X0) £	Corresponding quarter (1/X0 – 3/X0) £
Month 1	15,600	17,200	16,200
Month 2	17,100	18,400	16,800
Month 3	17,250	17,500	16,000
Total	49,950	53,100	49,000

Answer 11

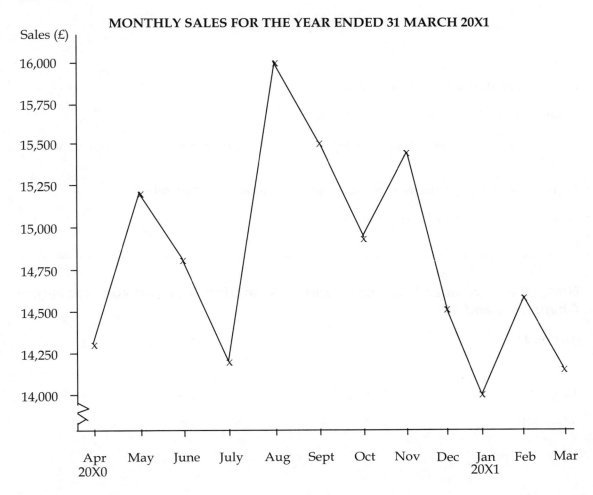

MONTHLY SALES FOR THE YEAR ENDED 31 MARCH 20X1

Answer 12

Task 1

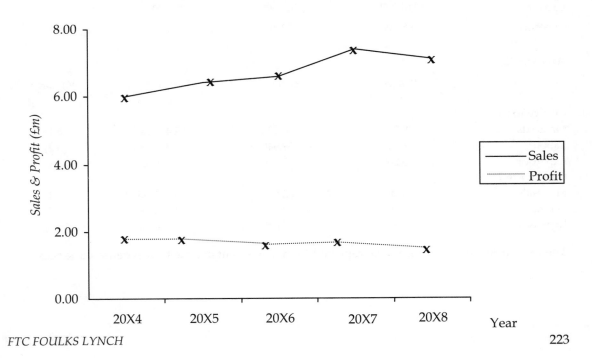

Graph of performance of Paper Products Ltd

Task 2

NOTEPAD

Profit increased between 20X6 and 20X7.

Profit has fallen by 26% between 20X4 and 20X8.

The profit fall cannot be caused by a fall in sales, as these have risen by 18% over the same period.

Therefore the fall in profits must be caused by costs rising faster than sales.

Total costs have risen by 37% over the period.

Budgeting, standard costing and information comparison (covering Chapters 9 and 10)

Answer 13

		£
Budgeted cost	2,600 kg × £3.40	8,840
Actual cost	2,700 kg × £3.40	9,180
		340 adverse

Answer 14

	April 20X1 £	April 20X0 £	Difference £	Difference %
Materials	253,400	244,300	9,100	3.7
Labour	318,200	302,600	15,600	5.2
Expenses	68,700	72,400	(3,700)	(5.1)

Answer 15

	Budget £	Actual £	Variance £	Variance %
Cost centre 1				
Materials	48,700	46,230	2,470 fav	5.1
Labour	37,600	39,940	2,340 adv	(6.2)
Expenses	5,200	3,700	1,500 fav	28.8
Cost centre 2				
Materials	56,200	62,580	6,380 adv	(11.4)
Labour	22,500	20,400	2,100 fav	9.3
Expenses	4,800	5,600	800 adv	(16.7)

The two variances which are to be reported to management are the two expense variances.

Answer 16

Task 1

Completed graph of the quarterly sales figures.

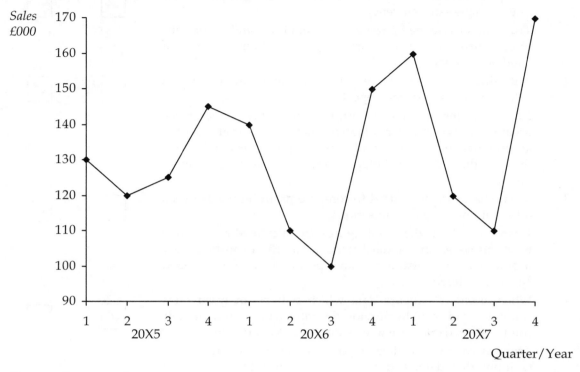

Comments on graph

The graph of quarterly sales figures is very irregular. Although the peaks in 20X6 and 20X7 are higher than 20X5, the troughs are also lower – it looks as if there's a trend for increasing sales.

Task 2

Budgeted sales revenue

Birmingham:	200 × £300 = £60,000
Cambridge:	150 × £300 = £45,000
Manchester:	180 × £300 = £54,000

Actual sales revenue

Birmingham:	206 × £285 = £58,710
Cambridge:	164 × £320 = £52,480
Manchester:	162 × £280 = £45,360

Completed sales variance report

	Birmingham £	*Cambridge* £	*Manchester* £
Budgeted sales revenue	60,000	45,000	54,000
Actual sales revenue	58,710	52,480	45,360
Variance	(1,290)	7,480	(8,640)

Cambridge is the branch with the most favourable results, as more units were sold than were budgeted for, and they were sold at a higher price than was budgeted for. Birmingham sold more units than budgeted, but at a lower price than budgeted. Manchester not only sold less units than was budgeted for, but also at a lower price than budgeted.

Task 3

		True	False
1	Before creating a pie chart to compare sales figures in all the European branches, Classic Pine Ltd should convert all the figures to the same currency.	✓	

True – otherwise the figures are meaningless. Millions of units of one currency may be worth only a few hundred units of another currency.

2	A deadline for an internal report is never more important than a deadline for an external report.		✓

False – if the internal report may influence whether the organisation goes into liquidation, and the external report is an optional survey for a trade association, for example, then the deadline for the internal report is obviously more important.

3	A bar chart cannot be used to compare profit figures between different units in an organisation.		✓

False – as long as the profit figures are calculated in the same way and stated in standard units, a bar chart can be a very useful way of illustrating how profit creation is divided between different units.

4	When asked to prepare data which will be analysed on a computer, you should provide the information on a suitable computer-readable format (eg a floppy disk), if possible.	✓	

True – if you provide data on paper, someone is going to have to input that data, and you can save time by inputting it yourself. In fact you may have already input it to prepare the paper copy, so it would then be sensible to provide both the paper copy and a copy on disk.

Spreadsheets (covering Chapter 11)

Answer 17

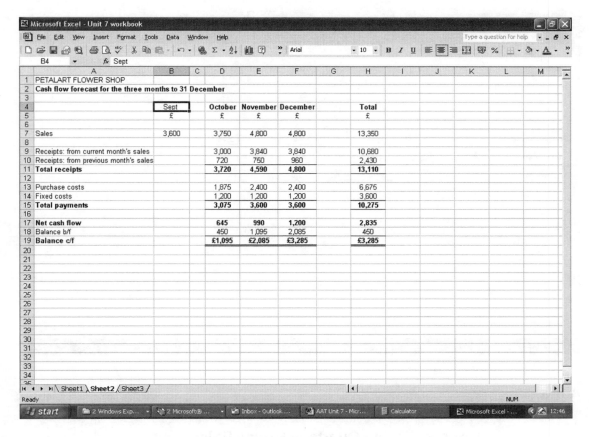

Note: formulae used (November column given as example)

E9:	=0.8*E7
E10:	=0.2*D7
E11:	=E9+E10
E13:	=0.5*E7
E15:	=E13+E14
E17:	=E11-E15
E18:	=D19
E19:	=E17+E18

If sales were to change as suggested in the query, the new balances can be computed by entering the new values in D7, E7 and F7 and letting the spreadsheet do the rest:

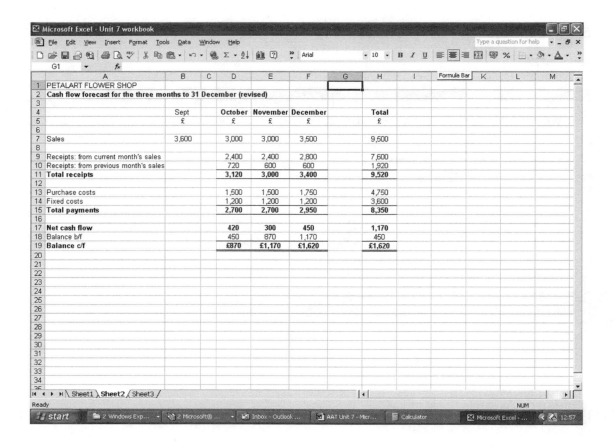

Answer 18

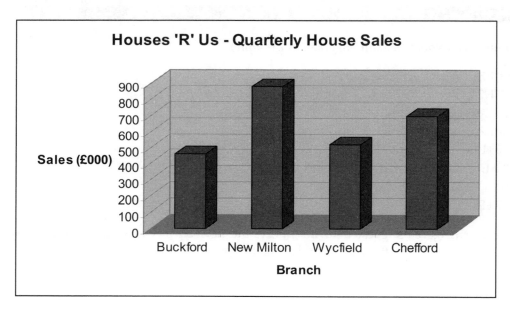

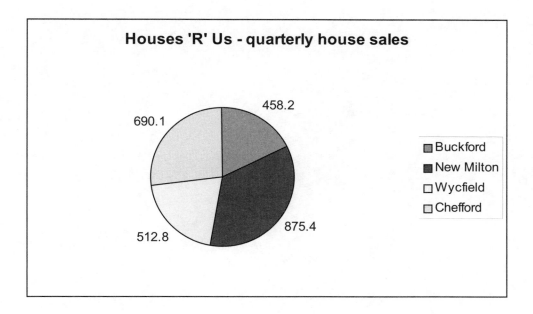

PRACTICE SIMULATION - ANSWERS

TASKS 1 AND 2

CODING EXTRACT – INCOME AND EXPENDITURE – AUGUST 20X3

(ROUNDED TO NEAREST £)

Code	Balance (£)	Amendment (£)	Updated balance (£)
111	38,916		
112	27,413		
113	33,476		
121	42,457		
122	29,376	1,700	31,076
123	24,294	3,800	28,094
131	38,461	1,600	40,061
132	34,761		
133	37,314	3,000	40,314
141	41,694		
142	52,316		
143	45,761		
211	47,412	750	48,162
212	11,467		
213	20,439		
221	43,764	890	44,654
222	11,461		
223	15,064		
231	8,216		
232	4,916		
233	9,074	1,500	10,574
241	3,642		
242	4,164	344	4,508
243	7,695	89	7,784
253	6,613		
263	7,008		
273	6,744		
283	4,539		

TASK 2

PAYROLL CALCULATION			
AUGUST 20X3			
NAME	John White		
DEPARTMENT	Packing		
BASIC RATE	£8.00 per hour		
HOURS WORKED	43		
HOURS FOR OVERTIME PREMIUM	8		
	Calculation	*Amount (£)*	*Code*
BASIC RATE	43×8	344.00	242
OVERTIME PREMIUM	$8 \times 8 \times 50\%$	32.00	243
EMPLOYERS PENSION CONT	$344 \times 6\%$	20.64	243
EMPLOYERS NIC	$(376 - 84)$ $\times 12\frac{1}{2}\%$	36.50	243
TOTALS FOR POSTING	*Code*		*Amount (£)*
	242		244.00
	23		89.14

TASK 3

MEMO

To: Liam Green

From: Candy Date

Date: 12 Sep 20X3

Subject: Invoice Coding

I have received the invoices you passed to me for checking and wish to make the following observations.

♦   The invoice from Ince and Sons has been coded as a printing department expense, however it was a charge for insurance for the factory as a whole. This needs to be apportioned to a range of departments and the basis for this can be discussed with Thelma, the management accountant.

♦   The invoice received from Aftercare Ltd was an invoice for a firm 'Cards Delight' in Portsmouth and not for our company. You need to draft a letter to them confirming the situation.

♦   The coding of the Cellplate Ltd invoice is correct, but there is an error on the invoice extension. Please check with the buying department, confirming the quantity ordered and the order price, before contacting Cellplate Ltd.

TASK 4

INCOME AND EXPENDITURE BALANCES – Year ending 31/12/20X3

Ledger account	Balance at 31/7/20X3 £	Amount coded August 20X3 £	Balance at 31/8/20X3 £
Sales			
Birthday cards			
- UK	245,365	38,916	284,281
- Europe	198,467	42,457	240,924
- USA	231,989	40,061	272,050
- Rest of World	297,946	41,694	339,640
Christmas cards			
- UK	246,578	27,413	273,991
- Europe	316,478	31,076	347,554
- USA	297,697	34,761	332,458
- Rest of World	399,906	52,316	452,222
Special Cards			
- UK	198,464	33,476	231,940
- Europe	201,897	28,094	229,991
- USA	246,890	40,614	287,204
- Rest of World	299,785	45,761	345,546
Expenditure			
Printing			
- Material	74,789	48,162	122,951
- Labour	61,890	11,467	73,357
- Expenses	93,167	20,439	113,606
Cutting			
- Material	71,789	44,654	116,443
- Labour	58,625	11,461	70,086
- Expenses	75,293	15,064	90,357
Wrapping			
- Material	58,693	8,216	66,909
- Labour	31,704	4,916	36,620
- Expenses	34,471	10,574	45,045
Packing			
- Material	38,568	3,642	42,210
- Labour	36,906	4,508	41,414
- Expenses	48,966	7,784	56,750

TASK 5

PERFORMANCE REPORT PRODUCTION COST CENTRES TOTAL COSTS – AUGUST 20X3			
	MONTH – AUG 20X3		YEAR TO DATE	
	Actual £	Budget £	Actual £	Budget £
Material	104,674	108,500	348,513	341,700
Labour	32,352	32,250	221,477	198,500
Expenses	53,861	48,750	305,758	277,100

TASK 6

DISCREPANCY (VARIANCE) REPORT PRODUCTION COST CENTRES AUGUST 20X3		
PERIOD / COST	MONTH £	YEAR TO DATE £
Material	3,826 F	6,813 A
Labour	102 A	22,977 A
Expenses	5,111 A	28,658 A

COMMENT

The significant variances which are more than 10% from budget are:

Month variances:	Expenses	£5,111 A
	Labour	£22,977 A
	Expenses	£10,002 A

TASK 7

SALES PERFORMANCE REPORT – AUGUST 20X3				
PERIOD / PROFIT CENTRE	MONTH ACTUAL	MONTH BUDGET	YEAR TO DATE ACTUAL	YEAR TO DATE BUDGET
	£	£	£	£
UNITED KINGDOM	99,805	98,000	790,212	785,000
EUROPE	101,627	109,000	818,469	832,500
USA	115,136	112,800	891,712	886,400
REST OF WORLD	139,771	142,100	1,137,408	1,164,000

TASK 8

NOTEPAD

Key points for telephone conversation with Sales Director:

♦ The report shows the performance relative to each profit centre.
♦ It shows performance for current month and the year-to-date.
♦ Actual and budgeted performance can be compared.
♦ Variances are shown to indicate favourable and adverse positions.
♦ Managers of the profit centres can be held accountable for the variances.

MOCK SIMULATION 1 ANSWERS

Task 1

ANALYSIS OF TURNOVER
WEEK ENDED 30 JUNE 20X2

Code	£
100.001	5,040
100.002	450
100.003	480
110.001	5,300
110.002	410
110.003	175
120.001	5,437
120.002	690
120.003	127
130.001	5,525
130.002	710
130.003	275
	£24,619

CODING EXTRACT - PURCHASES
WEEK ENDED 30 JUNE 20X2

(to nearest '£')

Code	£
100.162	3,250
100.165	5,850
110.155	140
110.156	450
110.162	3,410
110.165	6,150
120.162	3,517
120.165	6,350
130.162	3,323
130.165	5,950
130.174	100
130.184	95
130.197	2,500
	£41,085

BATCH CONTROL SHEET - PURCHASE INVOICES
(show £ and pence)

	£
NE Fuel & Garages	15,862.50
Loftus Insurance Services	24,300.00
Raw Garage Supplies	117.50
Filey Office Supplies	528.75
PED Motor Supplies	111.62
NE Coast Trader	164.50
	£41,084.87

To nearest '£', agreeing with total purchases above	£41,085

Task 2

ANALYSIS OF TURNOVER, BUDGET – ACTUAL
PERIOD ENDED 30 JUNE 20X2

Code	Budget to 30 June £	Actual to 23 June £	Actual w/e 30 June £	Actual to 30 June £	Variance increase/ (decrease) £
100.001	120,000	122,500	5,040	127,540	7,540
100.002	11,000	12,300	450	12,750	1,750
100.003	12,000	12,100	480	12,580	580
110.001	132,000	129,400	5,300	134,700	2,700
110.002	10,500	9,500	410	9,910	(590)
110.003	5,000	4,100	175	4,275	(725)
120.001	135,000	131,200	5,437	136,637	1,637
120.002	15,100	14,900	690	15,590	490
120.003	3,100	2,750	127	2,877	(223)
130.001	130,000	126,000	5,525	131,525	1,525
130.002	16,100	14,800	710	15,510	(590)
130.003	5,125	4,100	275	4,375	(750)
	£594,925	£583,650	£24,619	£608,269	£13,344

% Total increase/(decrease)	2.24%

Task 3

TURNOVER, BUDGET – ACTUAL
% COMPARISON, PERIOD ENDED 30 JUNE 20X2

Code	Budget £	Actual £	% increase/ (decrease) (to 2 decimal places)
100.001	120,000	127,540	6.28
100.002	11,000	12,750	15.91
100.003	12,000	12,580	4.83
110.001	132,000	134,700	2.05
110.002	10,500	9,910	(5.62)
110.003	5,000	4,275	(14.50)
120.001	135,000	136,637	1.21
120.002	15,100	15,590	3.25
120.003	3,100	2,877	(7.19)
130.001	130,000	131,525	1.17
130.002	16,100	15,510	(3.66)
130.003	5,125	4,375	(14.63)
	£594,925	£608,269	2.24%

Task 4

WHITBY BRANCH
GROSS PAY WEEK ENDED 30 JUNE 20X2

Name	Basic hours £	Overtime £	Bonus £	Total £
J Smith	190	15	28	233
B Brown	190	75	28	293
J Dunn	190	75	28	293
P Jones	190	90	28	308
K Jones	190	30	28	248
J Martin	190	60	28	278
B Smithers	190	90	28	308
W Bows	190	90	28	308
J Stockdale	190	60	28	278
B Gull	190	15	28	233
	£1,900	£600	£280	£2,780

Coding analysis (to nearest £)

130.161	2,314	(drivers)
130.163	466	(reception and workshop)
	£2,780	

Bonus calculation : Turnover × 5% = £5,525 × 5% = £276.25

Bonus per employee : $\frac{£276.25}{10\,employees}$ = £27.63 = £28 to the nearest £

Task 5

SUMMARY OF GROSS WAGES TO DATE
- 30 JUNE 20X2

Code		£
100.161		57,100
100.163		6,100
110.161		58,250
110.163		5,875
120.161		59,100
120.163		5,975
130.161	(54,650 + 2,314)	56,964
130.163	(11,600 + 466)	12,066
		£261,430

TASK 6

ANALYSIS OF GROSS WAGES, BUDGET – ACTUAL
PERIOD ENDED 30 JUNE 20X2

Code	Budget	Actual	Variance increase/ (decrease)	% increase/ (decrease)
	£	£	£	%
100.161	55,000	57,100	2,100	3.82
100.163	6,000	6,100	100	1.67
110.161	58,000	58,250	250	0.43
110.163	5,900	5,875	(25)	(0.42)
120.161	59,500	59,100	(400)	(0.67)
120.163	5,750	5,975	225	3.91
130.161	57,500	56,964	(536)	(0.93)
130.163	12,000	12,066	66	0.55
	£259,650	£261,430	£1,780	0.69%

Task 7

MATERIAL REQUISITION CODING
WEEK ENDED 30 JUNE 20X2

Coding	£
100.165	15.00
110.155	22.50
120.155	11.50
130.165	3.00
	£52.00

Task 8

PETTY CASH VOUCHER ANALYSIS
WEEK ENDED 30 JUNE 20X2

Bridlington branch

Coding	£
100.153	21.50
100.155	37.00
130.197	3.50
	£62.00

Task 9

CRESCENT TAXIS LTD

MEMO

To: All branch receptionists

From: Jarem Zareere

Date: 30 June 20X2

Subject: Petty cash vouchers

I have noticed on recent visits to branches that certain petty cash vouchers have not been signed by either the person requesting the payment or the receptionist responsible for authorising the payment.

It is essential that all payments are signed twice both for request and authorisation.

As a limited company we are subject to audit and the need to maintain proper internal controls. If such omissions are noted by the auditors they will report this to the owner/director.

Please ensure that this important requirement is adhered to.

I shall note particular attention to this on my next visit.

Many thanks.

Jarem

CRESCENT TAXIS LTD

MEMO

To: Bill Gull

From: Jarem Zareere

Date: 30 June 20X2

Subject: Material requisitions

The central stores function was introduced to control the issue of both maintenance and other indirect materials issued to branches.

I have noticed recently that certain requisition forms have not been signed.

In order to make staff and branches receiving materials accountable for the expenditure, we need to ensure that such issues are both signed for request and authorisation.

Please ensure that this occasional omission is not repeated in future.

Many thanks.

Jarem

Task 1

INVOICE

Fantastic Frames

Invoice to: E L Salons 20 Rueja Alta Madrid SPAIN	Bridge Park Estate Wallingham NT16 4LP Tel: 0488 611 202 Fax: 0488 611 203

Invoice no:	26719
Tax point:	30 June 20X1
VAT reg no:	384 6113 97

Code	Description	Quantity	VAT rate %	Unit price £	Amount exclusive of VAT £
G12P	Gilt Frame	250	17.5	16.40	4,100.00
S07A	Silver plate frame	180	17.5	9.20	1,656.00

			5,756.00
VAT at 17.5%	**Code:** 20313 20311	**£** 4,100.00 1,656.00	1,007.30
Total amount payable			6,763.30

INVOICE

Fantastic Frames

Invoice to:
Humbug Stores
Victoria Place
Wilton
Cheshire
England

Bridge Park Estate
Wallingham
NT16 4LP
Tel: 0488 611 202
Fax: 0488 611 203

Invoice no:	26720
Tax point:	30 June 20X1
VAT reg no:	384 6113 97

Code	Description	Quantity	VAT rate %	Unit price £	Amount exclusive of VAT £
W61T	Wood frame	40	17.5	18.80	752.00
S11L	Silver plate frame	25	17.5	12.60	315.00
					1,067.00

VAT at 17.5%

Total amount payable

Code:	£
20112	752.00
20111	315.00

186.72
1,253.72

INVOICE

Invoice to:
Fantastic Frames
Bridge Park Estate
Wallingham
NT16 4LP

T J Wood Supplies

Porter House
Wallingham
NT4 6NT

Invoice no: F4712
Tax point: 27 June 20X1
VAT reg no: 462 3779 14

Code	Description	Quantity	VAT rate %	Unit price £	Amount exclusive of VAT £
PT410	Stripped Pine	140 m	17.5	6.25	875.00
M2623	Mahogany	85 m	17.5	9.20	782.00
					1,657.00

VAT at 17.5%

Total amount payable

Code:	£
10121	1,657.00

289.97

1,946.97

INVOICE

Specialist Paints

Invoice to:
Fantastic Frames
Bridge Park Estate
Wallingham
NT16 4LP

28/32 Upper Street
Fairborough
NT23 0LP

Invoice no:	6124
Tax point:	26 June 20X1
VAT reg no:	442 3791 88

Code	Description	Quantity	VAT rate %	Unit price £	Amount exclusive of VAT £
2461	Gold Paint	20 litres	17.5	15.80	316.00

		316.00
VAT at 17.5%		55.30
Total amount payable		371.30

Code:	£
10321	316.00

Tasks 2 and 3

Coding extract – income and expenditure – June 20X1 (Rounded to the nearest £)

Code	Balance £	Amendment £	Updated balance £
10121	76,395	1,657	78,052
10122	24,576		
10123	8,146		
10221	13,574		
10222	64,685	395	65,080
10223	9,326	96	9,422
10321	23,465	316	23,781
10322	57,689		
10323	6,275		
10421	18,765		
10422	15,781		
10423	10,367		
10522	18,254		
10523	3,255		
10622	19,370		
10623	4,174		
10722	70,325		
10723	26,485		
10822	61,350		
10823	57,385		
20111	95,327	315	95,642
20112	86,790	752	87,542
20113	88,264		
20211	67,375		
20212	71,484		
20213	62,549		
20311	54,185	1,656	55,841
20312	39,265		
20313	42,465	4,100	46,565
20411	18,478		
20412	20,365		
20413	17,363		

Task 3

Payroll calculation schedule – June 20X1			
NAME	Lillian Frant		
DEPARTMENT	Assembly		
BASIC RATE	£9.40 per hour		
TOTAL HOURS WORKED	42 hours		
OVERTIME HOURS WORKED	7 hours		
	Calculation	**Amount £**	**Code**
BASIC PAY	42 × £9.40	£394.80	10222
OVERTIME PREMIUM	7 × £9.40 × $\frac{1}{2}$	£32.90	10223
EMPLOYER'S PENSION CONT.	5% × £394.80	£19.74	10223
EMPLOYER'S NIC	(394.80 + 32.90 – 84.00) × 12.5%	£42.96	10223
TOTALS FOR POSTING (£)		£395	10222
		£96	10223

Task 4

Coding extract – income and expenditure – year to 30 June 20X1 (Rounded to the nearest £)

Code	Balance at 31 May £	June figures £	Updated balance at 30 June £
10121	228,310	78,052	306,362
10122	71,254	24,576	95,830
10123	24,165	8,146	32,311
10221	38,450	13,574	52,024
10222	193,272	65,080	258,352
10223	27,364	9,422	36,786
10321	69,264	23,781	93,045
10322	171,264	57,689	228,953
10323	18,325	6,275	24,600
10421	55,163	18,765	73,928
10422	42,673	15,781	58,454
10423	28,663	10,367	39,030
10522	56,264	18,254	74,518
10523	9,265	3,255	12,520
10622	57,265	19,370	76,635
10623	12,574	4,174	16,748
10722	209,436	70,325	279,761
10723	78,412	26,485	104,897
10822	183,562	61,350	244,912
10823	172,563	57,385	229,948
20111	296,385	95,642	392,027
20112	258,233	87,542	345,775
20113	264,264	88,264	352,528
20211	201,573	67,375	268,948
20212	215,265	71,484	286,749
20213	186,254	62,549	248,803
20311	158,325	55,841	214,166
20312	117,637	39,265	156,902
20313	127,254	46,565	173,819
20411	53,672	18,478	72,150
20412	60,261	20,365	80,626
20413	47,365	17,363	64,728

Task 5

Performance report – production cost centres – total costs				
June 20X1				
	Month – June 20X1		Year to date	
	Actual £	Budget £	Actual £	Budget £
Materials	134,172	120,350	525,359	476,900
Labour	163,126	170,560	641,589	722,400
Expenses	34,210	31,600	132,727	130,500

Task 6

Variance report – production cost centres – June 20X1		
	Month £	Year to date £
Materials	13,822 A	48,459 A
Labour	7,434 F	80,811 F
Expenses	2,610 A	2,227 A

Comment

Materials – June variance	11.5% A
Materials – year to date variance	10.2% A
Labour – year to date variance	11.2% F

Task 7

Sales performance report – June 20X1				
	Month – June 20X1		Year to date	
	Actual £	Budget £	Actual £	Budget £
United Kingdom	271,448	290,500	1,090,330	1,250,000
France	201,408	190,300	804,500	740,200
Spain	141,671	120,000	544,887	440,000
Rest of Europe	56,206	61,200	217,504	200,000

Task 8

Variance report – sales – June 20X1		
	Month £	Year to date £
United Kingdom	19,052 A	159,670 A
France	11,108 F	64,300 F
Spain	21,671 F	104,887 F
Rest of Europe	4,994 A	17,504 F

Comment

United Kingdom – year to date variance	12.8% A
Spain – June variance	18.1% F
Spain – year to date variance	23.8% F

Task 9

Sales analysis report – June 20X1

	Month – June 20X1		Year to date	
	Actual £	Budget £	Actual £	Budget £
Silver plate frames	237,336	213,000	947,291	895,000
Wood frames	218,656	235,000	870,052	950,000
Gilt frames	214,741	194,000	839,878	755,000

Task 10

Variance report – sales analysis – June 20X1

	Month £	Year to date £
Silver plate frames	24,336 F	52,291 F
Wood frames	16,344 A	79,948 A
Gilt frames	20,741 F	84,878 F

Comment

Silver plate – June variance	11.4% F
Gilt – June variance	10.7% F
Gilt – year to date variance	11.2% F

Task 11

NOTEPAD

♦ Sales report by profit centre shows the income of each designated profit centre of the business.

♦ The performance of each profit centre can be measured against budget by supplying the variances from budget.

♦ Variances can be calculated showing favourable and adverse performance.

♦ Profit centre managers can be asked to explain the variances.

♦ Sales report by product shows how the sales of each product compare to the budgeted sales for each type of product.

♦ Trends in sales can be illustrated by changes in relative sales between each type of product.

♦ Both of use but providing different information – the sales report by profit centre may be more useful as this is the manner in which the performance of the organisation can be judged.

Index

FTC Foulks Lynch
A **Kaplan Professional** Company

STUDY TEXT/WORKBOOK REVIEW FORM
(AAT Unit 4)

nk you for choosing this FTC Foulks Lynch Study Text/Workbook for your AAT qualification. As we are
tantly striving to improve our products, we would be grateful if you could provide us with feedback about how
ul you found this publication.

ie: ....

ess: ....

....

il: ....

did you decide to purchase this
ly Text/Workbook?

		How do you study?	
e used them in the past	☐	At a college	☐
ommended by lecturer	☐	On a Distance Learning Course	☐
ommended by friend	☐	Home study	☐
advertising	☐	Other (please specify)...	

r (please specify)...

in our AAT range we also offer Distance Learning Courses and Pocket Notes. Is there any other type of
ice/publication that you would like to see as part of the range?

Rom with additional questions and answers ☐

oklet that would help you master exam skills and techniques ☐

ce on our website that would answer your technical questions and queries ☐

r (please specify)...

ng the past six month do you recall seeing/receiving any of the following?

advertisement in *Accounting Technician* magazine? ☐

leaflet/brochure or a letter through the post? ☐

r (please specify)...

rall opinion of this Study Text/Workbook

	Excellent	*Adequate*	*Poor*
ductory pages	☐	☐	☐
dards coverage	☐	☐	☐
ity of explanations	☐	☐	☐
ity of definitions and key terms	☐	☐	☐
grams	☐	☐	☐
ities	☐	☐	☐
k quiz questions	☐	☐	☐
technique questions	☐	☐	☐
wers to key technique questions	☐	☐	☐
k exams/skills tests	☐	☐	☐
ut	☐	☐	☐
x	☐	☐	☐

u have further comments/suggestions or have spotted any errors, please write them on the next page.

se return this form to: Veronica Wastell, Publisher, FTC Foulks Lynch, Swift House, Market Place,
Wokingham, Berkshire, RG40 1AP, United Kingdom

Other comments/suggestions and errors

AAT Order Form

Swift House, Market Place, Wokingham, Berkshire RG40 1AP, UK.
Tel: +44 (0) 118 989 0629   Fax: +44 (0) 118 979 7455
Order online: www.financial-training.com
Email: publishing@financial-training.com

...er your books, please indicate quantity required in the relevant order box, calculate the amount(s) in the column, and add postage to determine ...nount due. Please clearly fill in your details plus method of payment in the boxes provided and return your completed form with payment attached.

...assessments in 2004/05	Study Text		Workbook		Pocket Notes		Amount
	Price £	Order	Price £	Order	Price £	Order	£
...ATION LEVEL							
Receipts, payments and an initial trial balance	20.00	☐	20.00	☐	6.00	☐	
	Study Text & Workbook						
	Price £	Order					
Supplying information for management control	15.00	☐					
...& 23 Working with computers, personal effectiveness and health & safety	15.00	☐					
...MEDIATE LEVEL	**Study Text & Workbook**						
	Price £	Order			Price £	Order	£
Maintaining financial records and preparing accounts	20.00	☐			6.00	☐	
Recording and evaluating costs and revenues	20.00	☐			6.00	☐	
Preparing reports and returns	20.00	☐					
...ICIAN LEVEL	**Study Text & Workbook**						
	Price £	Order			Price £	Order	£
Performance management, enhancement of value and planning & control of resources	20.00	☐			6.00	☐	
Managing systems and people in the accounting environment	15.00	☐					
Drafting financial statements	20.00	☐			6.00	☐	
Cash management and credit control	15.00	☐			6.00	☐	
Implementing auditing procedures	15.00	☐			6.00	☐	
Business taxation (FA03)	15.00	☐			6.00	☐	
Business taxation (FA04)	15.00	☐			6.00	☐	
Personal taxation (FA03)	15.00	☐			6.00	☐	
Personal taxation (FA04)	15.00	☐			6.00	☐	
...et Notes for Units 1, 2, 3 & 4 are published in one book							
...et Notes for Units 6 & 7 are published in one book					**TOTAL**		

...e, Packaging and Delivery (per item):

...Texts and Workbooks	First	Each Extra	Pocket Notes		First	Each Extra
	£5.00	£2.00	UK		£2.00	£1.00
...e (incl Republic of Ireland and Channel Isles)	£7.00	£4.00	Europe (incl Republic of Ireland and Channel Isles)		£3.00	£2.00
...* World	£22.00	£8.00	Rest of World		£8.00	£5.00

...ct Sub Total £...................	Postage & Packaging £.................	Order Total £..................	(Payments in UK £ Sterling)

...mer Details

☐ Mrs   ☐ Ms   ☐ Miss   Other ....

.... Surname: ....

...ss: ....

....

....

...de: ....

...ry Address – if different from above

...ss: ....

....

...de: ....

...one: ....

....

...ry please allow:–	United Kingdom	– 5 working days
	Europe	– 8 working days
	Rest of World	– 10 working days

Payment

1   I enclose Cheque/Postal Order/Bankers Draft for £.....................................

Please make cheques payable to '**The Financial Training Company Ltd**'.

2   Charge MasterCard/Visa/Switch no:

Valid from: |__|__|__| Expiry date: |__|__|__|

Issue no:

(Switch only) |__|__|

Signature: .... Date: ....

Declaration

I agree to pay as indicated on this form and understand that The Financial

Training Company's Terms and Conditions apply (available on request).

Signature: .... Date: ....

Notes: All orders over 1kg will be fully tracked & insured. Signature required on receipt of order. Delivery times subject to stock availability. A telephone number or email address is required for orders that are to be delivered to a PO Box number.